You Can Know GOD Personally

Inspiring Stories *and* Essays *for* Everyone

Charlie Burr

ISBN 979-8-88751-913-5 (paperback)
ISBN 979-8-88751-914-2 (digital)

Christian Faith Publishing
832 Park Avenue
Meadville, PA 16335
www.christianfaithpublishing.com

Printed in the United States of America

Contents

STORIES

My Worst Day Soon
Became My Best Day

It was 3:00 p.m., Wednesday, February 14, 1962, in Arcadia, California. Yes, Valentine's Day. Back then, even in sixth grade, we children gave each other valentines and enjoyed a class party. Carrying them under my arm, this twelve-year-old boy, Charlie Burr, walked to the front of his school to catch the school bus home. I was happy, content, and ready to relax.

The next moment sent shock waves through my body. Parked behind the bus were my mom and my paternal grandfather in the same car. Mom and Dad had bitterly divorced when I was only three years old, so seeing these two people together was a strange sight. Mom was curling her forefinger in a "Come here" motion. She looked dead serious as I walked toward the car. I knew something was up—something bad.

"Get in," was all I heard as I opened the back door. We drove off in silence, but a few minutes later, Mom said coldly, "You're going to go live with your father in Phoenix. You'll have ten minutes to pack."

I started objecting and crying, but with my grandpa in the front seat, I could tell that this was a done deal, well planned earlier in the day. Grandpa was going to take me with him as soon as I could get ready.

Back at home for the final time, I sobbed as I threw some clothes into a suitcase, begging my mom not to send me away. She was adamant, however, and kept urging me to hurry up. I had no time to say goodbye to my dog or cat in the backyard. I left my rock, stamp, and baseball card collections behind as I quickly packed. Soon, Mom said a polite goodbye as she closed the front door behind me, and I began a miserable walk to the car. I got in, feeling as though my world had been turned completely upside down in a matter of minutes. Grandpa started the ignition. It would be the last time that I would ever see the inside of that house. I was beyond crushed. I had been totally rejected without any explanation.

During the mostly silent drive, Grandpa told me that he was merely taking me to his own house in nearby Claremont, and then my dad would drive over from Phoenix (350 miles away) to pick me up the following weekend. I couldn't bear the idea of never seeing my school friends again or the thought of the bewilderment they would experience from looking at my empty desk the next several days. They would probably find out soon enough that Charlie was never coming back, and there must have been something mysteriously bad about him for that to have happened. So I began to fear even further rejection on top of what I already felt.

And what would become of my pets? Would they be gone before long? Would Mom give them away or simply take them to the pound? If she did either one, then there was no possible way I would ever get to see them again. In my mind, I kept trying to picture how they looked. I wished I'd been allowed just one minute to pet them.

Valentine's Day is supposed to be a happy occasion, full of warm, heartfelt expressions, with cards, candies, and even a special dinner. It is surely one of the worst days to feel completely abandoned. As the day progressed, I kept thinking, *If I can only talk to Mom and promise her what a good boy I'll be, then she'll take me back. I'll plead with her.*

As we talked, however, my grandpa made it clear to me that she had made a final decision. My mom didn't want me anymore and had decided that it was time for me to live with my dad. So this new reality was beginning to set in, leaving me in tears the whole way. This can't be happening, but it definitely *was* happening. It must be someone else going through this, but actually, it's me. My old life was rapidly disappearing, minute by minute, never to return. That's pretty hard for a twelve-year-old to withstand.

The next Saturday, my dad came to Claremont to get reacquainted with me and then to bring us back to Phoenix. Since the divorce, I had only seen him for two-week summer visits, so I didn't really know him that well. He had remarried, so this new life would involve getting along with my unfamiliar stepmother as well as with him. Was he glad to take me on? I think so but couldn't completely tell. I was still much too upset for the next several days even to consider my dad's own feelings. This would be a huge adjustment for him too. He could have said, "No." And where would that have left me? Years later, I'm very grateful that he said, "All right."

Before long, I was getting used to my new school, teachers, and classmates, plus the desert heat. Dad and Kay were treating me well. Still, every thought I had was of somehow returning to my mom. Then, unexpectedly, something unique took place on my first weekend in Arizona. After completing my initial week of school, I assumed that Saturday would be a fun, do-nothing kind of day. However, my dad let me know that he wanted to take me over to the children's choir practice at his church. Church? I'd never been to such a place before in my entire short life. Without arguing, I went along for the ride.

Upon entering the large choir room, something special took place. Ten to twenty kids my age were poised to start singing. Right away, I loved the songs, the sound, the group, and one thing more: I could sense that God was there, that he loved me, and that I desperately needed his love in my life for my broken spirit. This was February 24, 1962—a much better day than the fourteenth. I still remember the melody and lyrics to the very first song we practiced. It was titled "O Divine Redeemer" with words such as *prayer*, *mercy*, *pardon*, *sins*, and *Lord*. The lyrics were new, but I could quickly perceive what they meant. How could I know? No one had discussed them with me beforehand. We children simply sang the songs. Looking back now, I realize that God silently instilled in me what they were all about. He made me aware that these words were precious and true, even the first time I ever heard them.

I sang in that choir for seven years, and we always performed a weekly anthem in church. Sunday nights became a joy as well.

The teenagers would meet for Methodist Youth Fellowship, enjoying sloppy joes and potato chips for dinner, followed by a variety of meaningful activities. I wanted to show up every week, and my dad was so good to take me. He was turning my worst experience into the best one.

One summer evening, at age fourteen, I decided to read the entire New Testament. It took many nights, but when I reached the halfway point of the book of John, I became overwhelmed by who Jesus is. His wisdom, strength, kindness, and warm, caring nature got through to me. I put my Bible down and quietly said, "God, I need you. I'll do anything for you."

At that instant, his love, joy, and peace began to wash over me. I could feel the Holy Spirit flooding through my body for several minutes. Right then, I simply knew I was being born again. This wonderful, personal God was revealing himself to me. He was making himself known by coming into my heart and changing me forever. I was becoming a new person. From then on, God and I remained very close, and I grew as a believer. This kind of relationship is meant for everyone else as well. I discovered that God is not a distant entity. He is our Father, who waits for us to talk with him. Why would anyone miss out on such a great encounter?

I gradually forgave my mom and even lived with her for the last two years of college! During my senior year, I met my future wife, Becky. God's power healed me in so many ways. My damaged self-image slowly improved. The hurt that I suffered turned into empathy for others. I became a good listener and a people person too. And I always celebrate Valentine's Day. No sad memories. That's the day when God began to find me. I needed to meet him, though I never knew it. He found me even when I wasn't seeking him. I'm no one special. God loves you just as much as he loves me—with open arms!

God's Miracles in My Life

◆

I'm not bragging at all, but God has performed twenty-five miracles during my lifetime to help me. This is no credit to me. I'm not better than anyone else. These are not mere coincidences nor are they spectacular, eye-popping events. They took place over a fifty-year span of my life, saving me much grief and destruction. I wrote them down a few months ago and was overwhelmed by the total number. Perhaps there are even more than twenty-five, all of which God worked behind the scenes. If you can't think of any in your lifetime, then I would say to pick up your pen and reflect again. I'm not unique in any way.

I didn't notice most of these miracles at the time they occurred because I was too self-absorbed to include God in my thinking. Therefore, I missed out on being grateful and simply accepted my so-called good fortunes like a dumb animal. That's the amazing thing—God was blessing me even while I was forgetting him. More than that, even as I ignored him, he still cared about me so much that he'd keep on rescuing me—undeservedly. It hurts my heart now to think about it. How could anyone, especially God, steadily continue to help me out with no acknowledgment on my part? That's incredible love.

In 1973, when I was a twenty-three-year-old college senior, I met and dated the best woman I ever found—Becky Comstock from Culver City, California. We married a year later and started our teaching careers. Or so I thought. There was one little problem: I was failing as a classroom substitute teacher. After years of training, I realized I wasn't cut out for this job. However, I couldn't tell Becky, for fear of being a failure in her eyes and in mine as well. I began to picture myself as a college graduate with no future and no income. I was nearing the brink of ruining our first year of marriage with my poor choice for a career.

God was one step ahead of our huge problem though. In the fall of 1974, Becky put both of us on the substitute list for Culver City, her own school district while growing up. We were living in Canoga Park at the time, which was forty-five minutes away in the morning rush hour. So, in human terms, her idea didn't make much sense. We were already working for many closer schools trying for full-time employment.

Lo and behold, Culver City began to call us the most. Each of us worked two to three times a week, often driving in together. I soon got asked to substitute for PE teachers at the elementary level, grades 1–6. Becky had never heard of this particular position. It never existed when she attended school there. The job was only four years old, with a credentialed physical education specialist at each school. This was a rare program which most districts had never embraced nor could afford. I liked PE, so I took a few courses, read several books, and applied. The following summer, somehow, there were three openings out of the eight schools. William Marsh, principal at Farragut School, liked me and wanted me to work for him. I was on staff for the next sixteen years! I loved the job and gradually developed an excellent curriculum.

All a big coincidence? Or was God saving me so that one future day I would believe in his protection and providence? I say, if you cannot thank God for a miracle such as this, then what will you ever thank him for? I meet Becky of Culver City, we live in the San Fernando Valley, she gets me on a sub list far away that has a position we never knew existed, and three openings come up for a green young teacher with no PE training. Plus, a principal had watched me substitute teach and thought I did well, though I have no idea what impressed him. Does God favor some people more than others? Instead of that question, just believe in him and ask for his help. That question will fade away. I'm simply filled with wonder and gratitude years later. God definitely, dramatically intervened in my life many times. He will in yours.

A Second Career Miracle

My first full-time teaching job as a physical education specialist at Farragut Elementary School in Culver City was threatened several times. Every few years, a state budget crisis would hit, causing administrators to warn of the elimination of the elementary PE programs. Each time, however, teachers would persuade the school district to make the needed cuts in *other* areas of the budget.

Starting in 1991, the pressure became too great. This budget crisis was so severe that the district was compelled to cut art and music teachers, as well as physical education staff. In the spring of that year, I realized my sixteen years of teaching for Culver City were coming to an end. I knew I was a very good instructor, so I had no fears about finding another PE position elsewhere, in public or private schools. A classroom teacher at Farragut expressed to me, "I would be very worried having to search for another teaching job." For some reason, though, I experienced a peace throughout the whole process.

Perhaps I was too cocky. Nothing came through. Hmmm…this was not going to be so easy. Enter God. Interestingly, I had taught three siblings, whose parents lived nearby, but who attended a church in Pacific Palisades. I knew nothing of Pacific Palisades, a half-hour away up the coast. They told me about a small Christian school which their church had opened two years earlier where I might apply. I phoned the school but was informed they had no openings. Being thorough, in a stubborn kind of way, I phoned again two weeks later, and was now told that they *did* have an opening! The current PE teacher was about to go out on pregnancy leave. She had not been trying to have a child. The timing was miraculous. This sudden opportunity became my one and only offer, and it turned out to be the best one!

I had a wonderful experience at Calvary Christian School. The campus was near the beach, the classes were small, the air was clean, the surrounding hills were beautiful, and the parents were good to me. My fellow teachers were encouraging and highly qualified, with most of them holding master's degrees. People prayed so much for our school that you could actually sense the sweet Holy Spirit in the air. Visitors would comment on how different our children were from those at other schools. I knew why.

Finally, I was allowed to pray with my students daily. Often, I'd let the children pray aloud. I always knew that something had been missing in public school, even at the end of an exciting day. It was prayer. It was acknowledging God and thanking him. It was taking the focus off the physical and placing it on the spiritual for each class, if only for a minute. That made all the difference in the world.

At age sixty-two, I was laid off at the end of my twenty-first year. I could have taught longer, but it was time. My wife had recently gone through four surgeries for bone cancer and needed me at home. When she decided to retire that June, then it all made sense—I was supposed to end my career at the same time she did.

You might say that something good just falls in a person's lap and then his career takes off. Many would claim luck to be on their side. They *caught a break* or were *in the right place at the right time.* The word *luck,* however, is not in the Bible, yet God's plan for our lives is. So we face two choices: the world is governed by blind chance and randomness, or it is directed by God out of his great love. If each day is a matter of luck, then we will never need the Lord. However, if *he* is in control, then our hearts should be grateful for every blessing. I choose the latter because I know his record. He has protected me and provided for me so often—way beyond my miraculous jobs. "I'm a self-made person," you claim. Well, if God says, "I love you," then wouldn't saving my career be within his reach? I'd say it is.

Thankful for What?

I once heard a good definition of an atheist. An atheist is a person who, when his heart is full of gratitude for the good things in his life, has no one to thank. That's true, but sometimes I'm no better myself. I often wake up in the morning, stare at my bedroom ceiling for a while, and say nothing. It's the perfect opportunity to start the day right by thanking God for his blessings, but my mind draws a blank. At some point, as I'm staring away, I have to make a deliberate effort to initiate a conversation with the Lord. Difficult as that seems to be, God will soon respond by communicating with me as well. It always happens that way. I can choose to enter into his presence or simply decide to roll out of bed.

I'll get through the day by not acknowledging God at all, but the emptiness of that choice will eat away at me. If I *go* it alone, then sadly, the Lord might actually *leave* me alone. But why turn in that direction if I don't have to? Instead, I can look up at that ceiling, begin the morning by being grateful, and invite my heavenly Father in. All it takes is a few words that should come from my heart, which leads me to ask, "Thankful for what?" What have I forgotten, taken for granted, put on the back burner, or even ignorantly refused to give God credit for? And what are some of the great things he has done that I *do* remember? Perhaps I'll come up with a short list or quite a lengthy one. What does God deserve?

Of course, I'll start with my good health, my home, my son, my faith, my church family, good neighbors, food, clothing, career, long marriage, and the fact that I live in the greatest, free country. These are the blessings God has poured out on me for seventy-two years for no reason other than the fact that he loves me. I feel a general, subtle awareness of each one of these blessings on a daily basis. Most of us do to some degree. However, it goes deeper than that, for as I dwell on God's provisions, I discover his miracles of exact timing and supernatural intervention often shining through.

God has always been working in my life for my own good behind the scenes, whether I praised him or not. He did so even when I would turn my back on him. What kind of crazy love is that? How thick can I have been? I remember Jesus asking his disciples, "Are you so dull?" (Mark 7:18). That seems out of character for Christ because it sounds like the vernacular of the day. But it certainly describes me throughout my lifetime. Yes, I *was* that dull and still am. And whenever I *did* thank him, he never said, "It's about time!" He kept shaping the inner man, patiently changing me through compassion and grace. He was slow to anger, although he did chastise me for long stretches, always showing mercy in the end.

Now, whenever I focus on what I've been given, I'm overwhelmed with gratitude. God has done more for me than I realized at first glance. I recognize the uniqueness of my house as one example. I do know that wherever we live, God puts us there, expecting us to bloom where we're planted. It's a huge blessing to have shelter, which God provides, so that we can serve him joyfully. All right, here's our story.

In the winter of 1984, my wife, Becky, and I desired to move away from Culver City to a bit larger place in Westchester. After putting our home up for sale, we received one offer in four months. Remarkably, it passed escrow. But we couldn't find the right house. A new realtor intervened (not appropriate) and showed us the very one I'm now sitting in. It had an enormous ham radio antenna next door, but the sale price had been lowered because of that unsightliness. This worked out great for us. Twelve men from our church came over on a Saturday to help us move for free. The timing was perfect, and the antenna was removed several years later. We found ourselves in a beautiful community with caring neighbors, more blessed than we could have ever hoped for. God did it, and he does it often. So please thank him for your own blessings each day. It might be a longer list than you would have first imagined.

Becky's Radiance

In her second half of her life, my wife, Becky, became a great witness for the Lord Jesus. She did it in a natural, flowing manner that quickly caused people to tune in. She would transition from small talk to God talk with imperceptible ease. She would maintain the same exact calm tone, displaying no fear or stress. Her listeners never interrupted because it seemed as though she was talking about what she had just eaten for lunch. Her segues were so inoffensive that people would simply continue taking in her kind words and godly advice. It wasn't as though Becky was trying hard to convert anyone—she was merely sharing the significant, life-changing truths she had discovered over the years. There was no pushiness or confrontation in her approach, nor was there meekness or self-consciousness in her voice. She could be standing or sitting, sharing from her heart anywhere, anytime, completely relaxed. Yet her words were striking and bold. After all, she was broaching a subject that is usually left untouched.

What helped my wife in her conversations was an innate desire to treat everyone the same. Nobody was considered less important or less knowledgeable. I would watch people swell with confidence as she would address them. She showed so much respect, even for the little guy, that sometimes a person's posture would actually improve when receiving the unexpected attention directed their way. No one made people feel more special than Becky. Her humor, encouragement, full eye contact, and easy way of including God in so many exchanges were unforgettable. It's little wonder that she couldn't be stopped from speaking about faith. She caused her listeners to feel so good about themselves that they wanted to hear more. Sometimes, I would actually observe an individual silently realizing, "I think I really do agree about God's goodness. She's so positive and so winsome about it that I believe it too!"

I never possessed such a gift, but I admired hers. Becky was convincing without attempting to be so. What a natural! She wasn't born this way—the Holy Spirit gradually changed her. She gave her heart to the Lord and, from then on, spent much time reading through her Bible, praying deeply, meditating, journaling, and growing. She loved to sing all kinds of contemporary worship songs in church and at home. She took hundreds of notes on sermons she heard over forty years as a Christian. Additionally, her worn-out Bible contained her many comments, written next to the favorite verses she cherished.

No one is perfect. Becky spent many hours confessing to God her shortcomings, sins, hurts, and worries that were difficult to overcome. She knew that Jesus was not just a great man but had died to forgive her and to take her into heaven. She fully believed everything he taught. Because of that faith, she glowed with God's precious love. This became the love which she so often exuded toward friends, acquaintances, and strangers. Make no mistake—her own efforts to be nice to people were not sufficient. God supernaturally gave her an eagerness to care about each human being placed in her life. With my own eyes, I watched the Lord mold her personality, making her into a new creation. This transformation took place over many years, producing a gentle, patient woman who would strengthen your beliefs before you even knew what was happening. She made faith in God absolutely appealing.

So away with pride! Away with calling yourself *a good person*. Away with envy, jealousy, and judging others. Why not humbly ask God to *change* you so that he can *use* you? Our heavenly Father is not out to make you feel bad about yourself. Just the opposite—he loves you! You say, "I'm sorry," many times to people but never, ever to God? That's pride talking. Becky listened to Jesus's thinking and not her own. "Repent," he said. "Be forgiven," he told us. "This is my blood, poured out for you," he declared. And finally, "Love one another as I have loved you," he commanded. That was Becky at her very best.

Church Search

I t's hard to find the right church. At least that's what my wife and I discovered as we searched for the right ones for forty years. Along the way, we attended seven different churches, each one seeming to be the best home we could find at the time. I admire people who belong to the same church for fifty years. I wish that could have been us, but it was not meant to be. At times, a church will change, and members feel compelled to leave. Also, it's quite possible to outgrow your church due to your own spiritual growth. Additionally, God might lead you to a new site where you can use your talents more effectively.

Every church we belonged to was the best one for that phase of our lives. Each one had its strengths, and we were glad to participate and to serve. Never did we desire to church hop, nor did we expect to hang in a while and then move on if something went sour. We always intended to stay put and help out.

In 1977, Becky and I realized we had very few friends. We had been married for three years, and the only people we visited were our relatives. That was good for a time, but we were beginning to branch out. I had a strong church background as a teenager but fell away in college. Becky's background was Catholic, and she was used to attending mass at Christmas and Easter. We were starting to read the Bible together just as a Christian acquaintance was inviting us to her church's activities. We also began to attend a few Bible studies, sporadically, at various places. This slow process went on for five years.

As a Methodist growing up in Arizona, I was used to a large church. So we decided to join the two-thousand-member Methodist

Church in Santa Monica. Our baby, Jason, was baptized there in 1982, and we thought all was well. The problem was that we were growing. From here on, I can only speak the truth.

We would hear the Bible being quoted in the sermons yet we drove home feeling empty and unfed. Why? Gradually, we figured out that the messages only contained small amounts of the gospel, leaving us wanting much more. We also discovered that a big church was not for us. There were too many people, and we got lost in the crowd. So we sadly moved on only six months after becoming members.

I was interested in finding a church in which we could have small group fellowship all year. I knew that was the best way to make friends and to ask questions about the Christian faith. We were fairly new believers, and our inquiring minds were searching for answers. What better way is there to look for a church than in the phone book? Yes, really. In 1982, I came across University Christian Church in the yellow pages. The listing mentioned its weekly Wednesday night dinners and Bible studies. We tried it out, loved the entire atmosphere, joined within a year, made several lifelong friends, and initiated a prison ministry. In 1988, however, we felt the need for more worship time. We desired to hear the new praise and worship music and to sing for a half hour every Sunday. We wanted to learn some twentieth-century songs before the century ended. We knew we were missing out. There were other factors too.

So we started going to the nearby Los Angeles Assembly of God. They had left most of the wonderful old hymns behind. The guitar, bass, keyboard, and drums now prevailed, and the organ was put to rest. We learned at least fifty new songs, which I still burst out singing a cappella in my house today! The sermons were longer (forty minutes), and we learned the Bible more thoroughly than ever. Two more lifelong friends emerged. We stayed for seven years, introducing the prison ministry there as well.

When a new head pastor comes along, sometimes a church will go through a dramatic change, and that was our case. We tried to make it work but finally had to look elsewhere. We weren't unique at all.

Next, we attended a church in Culver City where we felt our thirteen-year-old son could fit in. His best friend was going there, so we had high hopes. Jason needed to be with his own age group. This effort lasted a year with moderate success. The service was quite different at times, with congregants being "slain in the Spirit" on the altar after the end of every sermon. Becky went up once, had her forehead pushed hard, and didn't fall backward as everybody else did. Needless to say, we didn't stay too much longer.

I was teaching physical education at a Christian school in Pacific Palisades and knew many parents, children, and teachers. The church there had started this ten-year-old school, and it seemed like a natural fit for Becky and me to join in. So we wound our way up the beautiful coast for a half hour on Sundays and enjoyed the contemporary service, the adult classes, the sermons, and the songs. Becky even joined the choir for a season. For four years things went well, but gradually, it became clear that I knew a lot of people, but Becky knew very few. I taught school there, but she only came once a week. I was used to the Palisades, but she felt a bit out of place. The drive was becoming too much for us as well.

In 2005, I drove past a church in Westchester right off the sidewalk. The marquee read, "Service at 11:00 a.m." I thought to myself, *Hmmm… I can make that.* Since I was now fifty-five and not very good at waking up early, this looked like an open invitation. So we tried out Hope Chapel, only five minutes from home, and liked it immediately. I had never met such outgoing, sociable people. Remarkably, the pastor spoke in the same friendly manner one-on-one as he did from the pulpit. He was personable and highly interactive—a real people person. We made a lot of friends through Bible studies and potlucks. God led us to pass out tracts in front of the church. Plus, I joined my very first men's group, which met every Monday night for eight years. I needed close male friends, and when times were rough, they prayed me through it. God answered their prayers. And when Becky returned home after major cancer surgeries, the women brought her meals for two months. We were overwhelmed by such generosity.

Yet in 2013, we just knew that we deeply desired to study the entire Bible, including the major prophets and Revelation. This wasn't going to happen at Hope. Somehow, God led us to Calvary Chapel LAX at a Thursday night service. We took a chance, went inside, and heard the book of Revelation being taught straight through for the first time in our lives! Pastor Dan Heard was bringing it to life over a sixth-month span. As we listened and kept coming back, Becky received two words about Calvary Chapel from the Lord. She often repeated these words to several people there: *honesty and purity*. This is what we needed at this stage of life—a church that taught every book of the Bible, verse by verse, with no rants or digressions. And when Dan Heard moved away in 2019, his place was taken by Justin Beck, who is the most positive, prepared pastor I've ever known. I'm never changing churches again!

There's no shame in joining a new house of worship. We were enriched by many different leaders, by all types of music, and by opportunities to serve. We weren't trying to use all seven churches for our own selfish purposes and then bolt at the first sign of trouble. We always wanted to find a home and to be a friend to those who needed us. Becky and I loved to extend ourselves to people and to take a personal interest in them. We were good listeners and encouragers wherever we went. We loved every church!

Passing Out Tracts Cheerfully

I t's pure joy to pass out tracts! How simple and easy it is to place the word of God into a stranger's hands. What took me so long to start doing it? I was once just as hesitant as anyone else.

In my thirties and forties, I admired Christians who were bold enough to leave a tract here and there. I would see them place one on a restaurant table or in a phone booth. I thought, *Maybe I could try that if no one would see me doing it.* Consequently, fear would get the best of me, and then I would go back to merely pondering the idea for a few more years.

In the 1990s, I went with a friend to an LA Laker's game then watched as he passed out tracts to the fans sitting around him when the contest ended. As he was handing out each one, he would simply say, "This is for you." Then he'd repeat the same phrase with the next fan. Everyone took a tract! Nobody turned him down. No one got nasty. I felt uneasy watching this scene unfold because I was struggling to gain confidence in myself. I was already convicted, but not yet victorious, over my worries of rejection. Instead of learning from my friend, I reacted with excuses and stayed far away from him later on when he invited me to go witnessing from door to door. That was way too advanced for a newbie.

At different churches I attended, I often hoped for a pastor to lead the way. I wanted the head guy to help ease me through this process. I needed a coach and a leader to follow. However, pastors are exceedingly busy doing the work God has called them to do, using the gifts he has given. I thought, *Well, shouldn't all of them be giving out tracts and setting an example?* In time, as I matured as an adult,

I came to realize that pastors might not be called to spearhead such activities or even have the hours available to do so. I was expecting too much. Unfortunately, at all these churches, nobody was passing out anything. There was no one around to show me the ropes.

About the time I turned fifty, I sensed the Lord's conviction so strongly that I just had to do something. I really wanted to share the gospel. I took a big chance and actually started placing some tracts on tables and in phone booths. I took an even bigger risk and handed out a few to cashiers while driving through fast-food restaurants. After all, how could they refuse a customer? And if they might get upset, I could always step on the gas. My heart would usually be pounding away, but I was gaining a bit of confidence.

In 2005, my wife, Becky, and I joined Hope Chapel in Westchester, a church which just happened to be right off a busy sidewalk. As I soon discovered, this was a great opportunity for a shy person to seize the moment. I could be on the sidewalk after the service and have the church sign right behind me to back me up! I felt emboldened by that sign and not so alone, which was my usual status. Plus, I could tell people, "That's my church behind me. Please come to the service next week. It's a friendly place, the pastor is wonderful, and the Bible is preached." At long last, I felt the assurance to face the public. Better yet, Becky decided to join me in this venture a few weeks later.

Oh yes, I had other fears to conquer along the way. What if somebody asks me a difficult question? What if I say the wrong words and accidentally turn someone off to Christianity? What if an individual gives me a hard time? And what if nobody ever takes a tract because I don't offer it winsomely? I found that these questions could only be answered by getting out there and gaining experience. The answers would follow after a step of faith. My wife and I would pray for God's direction, protection, and strength and that people we'd encounter would open their hands and receive the good news.

Every Sunday, the two of us would go outside for half an hour with several dozen small paperback copies of the Gospel of John, along with a Billy Graham tract titled *Steps to Peace with God* tucked inside. The two combined cost us fifty cents, which we gladly paid in order to spread the word. We would buy them in large quantities from a company called Crossway. In time, we tried other tracts as well. There are so many from which to choose, and Christians often have their favorites.

No matter what we offered up, we came to discover that people take them. What a thrill! We would pass out approximately thirty in thirty minutes. Our famous lines turned out to be, "Would you like the Gospel of John? It's a good book. It changed my life." That's not very creative but effective. Sometimes passersby would pause and discuss their beliefs or inquire about our church, wanting to know more about our faith. We would converse excitedly, encouraging them before they'd begin to move on. At other times, people were open, and we'd gladly pray for their salvation. However, we never tried to make folks stop because we wanted to keep distributing the literature. This became our best approach.

One of the most awesome moments in life is watching new contacts read a tract as they are walking away from me! You rejoice, you pray, and you thank the Lord that his message is spreading. What about those fear-based questions I wrestled with when I began? No one has really given me a hard time. No one has asked a question too tough. No one has yelled at me except for the homeless. Of course, things could always change. I'm ready to evangelize and to be kind and tactful during the interaction. I study books on apologetics extensively but hardly anyone seems interested in that subject. Nonetheless, I'm prepared just in case someone wants a short debate. And at times it doesn't hurt to say, "I don't know every answer, but can I get back to you?" That may happen as well.

Together, we felt drawn to the busy sidewalk. It was just crowded enough so that we could engage every pedestrian with a question or two. Our hearts would cry out for these thousands of individuals who were only a few steps away from entering a church! They were so close yet so far. Particularly, I was stirred by God with these observations: "How can I just keep on letting lost souls walk past my church? It's so sad. They are right there in front of me. How can I not reach out to them? There are so many. I don't even have to go searching. The truth is, quite often, they know that they need the Lord."

While this ministry is a way of emerging from the four walls, it is also a means of overcoming my perception of crowds as merely strangers in a metropolis. In the process, I've discovered that I'm helping myself as much as anyone else. I need to meet the public. It does my heart good to discover that a lot of people have heard of John's gospel. They recognize his name when I say it. He's not a complete mystery, and this is not a lost city, as some claim it is. There's a lot of hope to be found on the street. I grow as a person and become spiritually stronger through every witnessing opportunity.

Later on, Becky and I joined Calvary Chapel LAX when it took over the building. When she passed away in 2017, I went through a sad season, but after several months, I got back out on the sidewalk. Now I'm there almost every Sunday for forty-five minutes. If I stand around any longer, then it seems like a job instead of a joy. I hope that you, too, will discover what God has laid upon your heart to do to serve him. He's given each one of us a gift! There's no reason to wait for your church to support your efforts. Just the other day, while inside a Subway, I noticed two forlorn-looking men eating their sandwiches alone. As I handed each man the Ray Comfort comic tract, *Are You a Good Person?*, I said softly, "This is for you."

Church Three Times a Week?

I s it necessary to attend church three times a week? I get invited to Bible studies, prayer groups, community groups, and midweek services throughout the year. Realistically, if I tried to attend everything offered, burnout would become a real possibility. Yet some people ask, incredulously, "Once a week is enough for me or for anyone. How could you possibly want to go to church so often?"

I've heard that pointed question more than once. Well, I'm not a rarity. Many Christians appear at their churches several times weekly. They even stay half the day to help set up, clean up, teach, sing, usher, greet, serve coffee, or do security. I'm in awe because they freely give so much of themselves.

The real concern then becomes, "What can I do to serve the Lord by driving to these meetings?" I go because I want to encourage others, speak the truth, and contribute what I know about the Scriptures. In short, I feel blessed if I get to help someone during a Bible study or afterward. I find that taking a personal interest in people and refraining from just talking about myself is very important. Christians need such relationships, especially with friends who aren't in a hurry.

I enjoy learning about other's lives, often just by asking a few questions. That must be part of God's purpose for me because I love to patiently and actively pay attention and then respond. It's funny because I don't like to be outtalked yet I desire to listen. The trick is that I have a lot to say in response, usually with positive words to build people up. Believers could always do more to strengthen one another's self-esteem. We all need friends who will talk *with* us and not *at* us and who provide a great deal of thoughtful feedback as well.

Sometimes, I tire of surface-level conversations with those I've known for years. I'd much rather begin to connect in more depth, which presents the opportunity to grow closer. Okay, so what makes me so relational? It's because I enjoy conversing. I always want to bring out the best in people by getting to know them better. Plus, they bring out *my* best as well. They do that just by being my friend. The fact that God made me a *people person* tells me that I should use that gift for doing some good. That's why I look forward to so many small groups. It's where the people are, and it's also where the Holy Spirit is likely to dwell. Besides, have you noticed that nighttime TV is pretty boring? Compared to interacting with live human beings, it's even *more* boring. Watching too much of it can cure anyone's insomnia.

Your neighbors may wonder why you are drawn to church even *once* a week. See if they will get into your car and go with you to find out! I've invited two neighbors, but they haven't come along yet. But do you know a few surveys have revealed that many people would attend a church if they were simply asked by someone? It's true. I remember the story of a woman whose neighbor invited her fourteen different times. When she finally said "Yes," she remained with that church for life. So we never really know. We think the answer will undoubtedly be "No," but we can't say that for certain. In 1977, my wife and I were invited and then showed up at a Wednesday night Bible study. This happened way before we would ever give Sunday services a chance. We needed a more intimate setting to feel comfort-able. Try that. And if people turn us down, we can always ask if there is anything we could pray about for them!

If I could repay the many Christians who caused me to pause and question myself in the past, I would do it. They were not afraid, and sometimes they were persistent. The end result was that they got me to focus on my relationship with God. He tracked me down, thanks, in part, to their witness and concern. Over time, the Lord gave me a love for his Word, his people, and his various gatherings. I enjoy all the fellowship, and my heart and my allegiance surely belong to my terrific church, Calvary Chapel LAX.

ESSAYS

The Old Testament Is True

Have you ever heard of the Hittites? They were a group mentioned forty-six times in the Hebrew Bible or Old Testament (OT) but nowhere else in all literature. Therefore, scholars and historians considered the forty-six references to be mythological for referring to an ancient people who obviously never existed.

In the late 1800s, archaeologists discovered the vast buried Hittite Empire in what is now Turkey. It was three thousand years old and rivaled the Egyptian empire in its size and scope. The alphabet was deciphered, and the kings, conquests, and stone records of a superpower came to life. The critics were silenced.

The truth be told, skeptics, as well as believers in God, are often looking for a history book to confirm the Bible. They sometimes forget that the Bible is a history book too.

The same could be said of the Jewish king David of 1000 BC. He is written about only in the Hebrew Bible and nowhere else. Was his very existence doubted? Of course it was for many centuries. In 1993, however, an inscription in stone of King David's name was excavated in Israel. It dates to the time period of his life and resides in a museum today. Once again, the naysayers were proven wrong.

In fact, thousands of archaeological findings continue to confirm the authenticity of OT figures, cities, and sites as the years go by. Do you know of even one that ever disproved the Scriptures? Simply put: there aren't any or else we would be informed of them through the media immediately, if not sooner.

It was once believed that Moses, who lived in the thirteenth century BC, could not have composed books of the OT because

Hebrew writing had not developed. However, in 2010, discoveries of the oldest Hebrew pottery inscriptions from 1000 BC were reported. The language is much older than was once known.

One of the most baffling questions concerns the Jewish authors of the OT. Why would they make their own people look so bad? That just isn't done. From Genesis to Malachi, the Israelites commit the sins of polytheism and idolatry again and again. In the book of Exodus, they even desire to go back to Egypt to become slaves once more after God has delivered them from 430 years of servitude! And when they do leave Egypt, the promised land is only eleven days away. Yet it takes the Hebrews forty years to arrive.

Also, if the Exodus story is mere fiction, why would anyone write that his own people were ever slaves in the first place? Who would make that up? It's as demeaning as you can possibly get. Instead, the author should have suggested that they were artisans or merchants perhaps, but certainly not slaves!

We find no final triumph in the OT either. You would think it would be evident, but the Bible is simply an honest book. Even the great leader, Moses, the most outstanding figure in its historical narratives, is not allowed to walk into the promised land. The great Moses! If anyone deserved to enter after forty years of wandering, it would certainly be him. Yet his own sin prevented him from reaching the goal.

The OT ends with a small number of returning Jewish exiles struggling to rebuild a wall and a temple in Jerusalem. At the same time, they are being harassed on all sides by their enemies. No triumph at all.

What about the rulers of the land? In other nations, kings were presented as faultless. This is not so in the credible pages of Scripture. Continually, the prophets lament, "He did evil in the eyes of the Lord."

Even the greatest of them all, King David, could not escape harsh condemnation. During his reign, he committed adultery with Bathsheba and then planned the murder of her husband, Uriah the Hittite. David's successor, King Solomon, eventually took seven hundred wives, many of whom led him to worship foreign gods. He ignored God's clear desire for a man to form a monogamous relationship with one woman.

Here's the final scoreboard: the Northern Kingdom of Israel had nineteen bad kings and zero good ones. The Southern Kingdom of Judah had twenty bad kings and eight good ones. These records come from the OT itself, and not from any outside source. So 19–0 and 20–8. Those are bad and sad numbers.

The question remains: Why would the writers of the thirty-nine OT books come up with a story line which condemns their own people? Other kingdoms and empires have left behind *boastful* records of accomplishments for us to ponder and envy. They worshiped many detestable deities as well. Incredibly, the OT insists that there is only *one* God, that he has given his chosen people the law to follow faithfully, and that they have failed to do so. God beckons them to repent and be forgiven.

Always, the same unifying theme prevails throughout the pages: God's redemption of humankind. God loves us, and we are to love him. That's a completely unique concept not found in other religions. Just who do you believe imparted these precious, supernatural truths to the Jewish people, if not God?

There are well over three hundred prophecies in Scripture. Some have already been fulfilled, and others will be fulfilled in time. Isaiah is considered to be the greatest prophet of all. In his fifty-third chapter, he presents a person who is a sinless, submitted, sin-bearing, sacrificial, suffering servant. This individual cannot be the prophet himself or the nation of Israel. This person has committed no sin, gives himself up willingly, being dead, "I like a lamb to the slaughter," and dies as he "bore the sin of many." Obviously, Israel has never been sinless, does not submit to death willingly, and cannot forgive sin by making "intercession for the transgressors." Only a perfect individual can fulfill this prediction. Only the sinless one will do.

With an open mind, who do you think this person is? If you have not decided previously, then who is it that is being revealed? Isaiah actually describes his final physical appearance vividly one chapter before in verse 14: "His appearance was so disfigured beyond that of any man, and his form marred beyond human likeness." Both astounding prophecies, written approximately 700 BC, are rich in their graphic details. Perhaps you have not been exposed to Isaiah 53 at all. Sometimes this chapter is suppressed and never read aloud. One thing is certain however. It's a highly precise prophetic writing, authored long before the coming of Jesus Christ.

Finally, the Dead Sea Scrolls, discovered in 1947 inside Israel's caves, prove that the Hebrew Bible was never altered or rewritten. The scrolls contain the entire OT, except for the book of Esther, dating from the second century BC. Our earliest previously existing copies were from AD 900. The Dead Sea Scrolls take us back one thousand years earlier. The only changes over that time span are mostly spelling differences and minutiae. There are no differing themes or stories. The scrolls silenced many scoffers. If they will admit it, they can now trust the accuracy and reliability of the biblical texts.

There is much more evidence to present, but please review what you have just read. Let some of it sink in and strengthen your faith. You will sometimes encounter doubters, and God would love for you to defend the veracity of his word. It's powerful and true!

The New Testament Is True

Some people have the notion that major portions of the New Testament (NT) have been added on, deleted, or altered in some way. That's a strange idea considering the fact that a great deal more would have been changed as well. Jewish authors wrote the twenty-seven books of the NT between AD 50–90, not allowing enough time for myths, legends, or epics to develop after Jesus's crucifixion in the year 32.

In all four gospels, women were first to discover Jesus's empty tomb. The difficulty here is that in the first century, women could not even testify in a court of law. They were considered mere gossips and men's property. These eyewitness accounts *should* have been deleted. The gospels should read, "Trustworthy *men* found the empty tomb first." After all, aren't you trying to draw new male believers to your cause?

Women touched him, followed him, and knelt at his feet. Scandalous! Unheard of! Rabbis would never allow that to occur. Yet Jesus continually elevated the status of women throughout his ministry. Now how are you going to bring in faithful men to follow your new religion by writing down offensive details?

Jesus even walked straight through Samaria. Jews usually walked *around* Samaria, which entailed many more miles. No one wanted to be defiled by unclean half-breeds. Then he had the audacity to speak to a lone Samaritan woman at a well. Men did not do those things. Still, the story remains, as it is written.

So, too, the parable of the Good Samaritan in Luke is another jolting insult to Jewish sensibilities. Some people even accused *Jesus* of being a Samaritan. In the first century, such a remark was a racial slur.

Your new religion does not become appealing when you write that Jesus's disciples argued as to who among them would be the greatest. Then, when they ought to have been brave, they abandoned him upon his arrest. The disciples were accurately portrayed as fleeing cowards. Peter would later deny that he even *knew* Jesus. So who would want to follow a group of proven wimps in the years ahead?

The disciples never expected the resurrection. It's not a concocted story. A surprising reaction occurs in Matthew 28:17. This gospel is three verses from its ending when it states, "When the disciples saw the resurrected Jesus, they worshiped him; but some doubted." Some *doubted*? What a thing to say! How does this help your cause? Why wasn't that word deleted? Could the NT actually be valid? This kind of an honest account demonstrates that the disciples were not simply a band of gullible followers.

There's no positive spin in Mark either. In chapter 3, Jesus is accused of being "demon possessed" and "out of his mind." What terrible insults! How do such criticisms promote your leader's public image?

And John 6:51–59 presents an even larger problem. In these verses, Jesus says four times to eat his flesh and drink his blood. However, Leviticus 17:10–14 commands the Hebrews to have nothing to do with blood. Do not drink it, and drain it out of all animals that you are going to eat. This was part of the law. The point is that no first-century author would ever write such words unless Jesus actually spoke them. Who would ever make up such an abominable command? A total turnoff to future Jewish believers!

Let's go on to his miracles. They are never embellished or flamboyant, as are the miracles in mythology. Instead, they are always simply stated, and then the writers invariably moved on. Also, the NT is written as a narrative, with thousands of details not found in fictional works of the time. For instance, in John 11:39, Lazarus has been lying dead for *four* days before Jesus *finally* approaches the town of Bethany. Showing strong compassion, Jesus weeps *convulsively* at Lazarus's tomb before raising his friend to life!

I once heard that Christianity is the only religion which has, as its main event, the humiliation of its God. Let's ponder that. It's quite true. What other religion would ever dare to allow its god to be slapped, spit on, blindfolded, beaten, mocked, whipped, nailed, and speared? How unthinkable that would be.

Were any serious ideas about Jesus added to the NT? No. He was called Christ and Lord in the early church's hymns, creeds, and prayers. See 1 Corinthians 15:3–8, 16:22, Philippians 2:6–11, and 1 Timothy 3:16. It becomes difficult to argue that Jesus was awarded those titles decades later for false purposes.

But here is a fictitious verse that *could* have been added. Matthew, Mark, and Luke all share an amazing prophecy coming from Jesus's own lips as he beheld King Herod's twenty-story Jerusalem temple, which required eighty-three years to construct: "I tell you the truth, not one stone here will be left on another; every one will be thrown down" (Matthew 24:2). Some of these "stone(s)" were forty feet long, twenty feet wide, and fifteen feet high, weighing eight hundred thousand pounds! This beautiful structure was thought to be indestructible.

Now Matthew loved to write about fulfilled prophecy in his book. He took every opportunity to do so. We all know what happened. Within forty years of Jesus's resurrection, Roman soldiers destroyed the temple, and today, anyone can travel to Jerusalem to view those giant, scattered, carved stones at ground level. Wouldn't it have been tempting to tack on a verse such as this to Matthew's account? "And Jesus's words were fulfilled when the temple was torn down." But nobody ever did! Not the disciples nor the early church nor the second-century church. Why not? Would it be accurate to say that the early Christians respected Matthew's book enough to leave it in its original form? Yes, exactly.

Jesus was unique. Often, he would declare, "I tell you the truth…" or "Truly, truly, I say unto you…" Well, what if he really meant it? What if every word he spoke *was* total truth without any deception? That would make his pronouncements even more credible, causing us to take him much more seriously.

Differing from all other rabbis, Jesus frequently stated, "But *I* say to you…" and "It is written…" as he quoted from Genesis, Exodus, Isaiah, etc. He spoke as *the* authority as he went about confirming the Hebrew scriptures. He took all OT stories literally, even Jonah and Noah, the two we often question.

When people worshiped him, Jesus never said, "No, stop. You've gone too far." Nor did he tell Pilate, "Look, my disciples just got carried away. I'm not the Messiah—only a teacher." In fact, at one of his six trials, he firmly stated, "I am" (Mark 14:62) when asked if he *was* the Messiah. Exodus 3:14 clarifies what those significant words indicate. God said "I am" to Moses. Jesus was declaring himself to be God.

Next, he spoke boldly of the future: "And you will see the Son of Man (Jesus) sitting at the right hand of the Mighty One (God) and coming on the clouds of heaven (The Second Coming)" (Mark 14:62). Only a liar or a psychotic would speak this way, and Jesus is neither. His promises are trustworthy and reliable.

The men who questioned him knew what he was claiming. At once they condemned Christ for blasphemy and were soon shouting for his death. Instead of easily escaping, Jesus chose to hang on a rough wooden cross for six hours. Three days later, he rose from the dead, opening the entrance of heaven to us for eternal life. He forgave all mankind for its wrongdoing—past, present, and future. Every person has sinned against a just and holy God, but God came to earth as a man—a sinless man who took the punishment for you and me. He paid the price and calls for us to repent and to ask for God's forgiveness. He invites us to believe him, receive him, and ask him into our lives today. God will fill you with his love, joy, peace, and purpose if you'll say, "Yes." It will be the best decision you can ever make!

Way Ahead of Its Time: Strong Evidence that This Bible Is Medically and Scientifically Accurate

In 1799, ex-president George Washington was a healthy sixty-seven-year-old, living in retirement on his Virginia estate. One night in mid-December, he awoke with a sore throat and breathing difficulty. His doctors were called, and they soon began the standard procedure of bloodletting to help him get well. Today, this practice seems bizarre and diabolical, but it was a common treatment for hundreds of years, even up through the 1800s. Doctors usually carried bleeding kits in their bags. Hoping to cure him, they did a thorough job on our famous president, draining eighty ounces of his blood. This comes to five pints, which is more than half a gallon, or 40 percent of Washington's blood. By the next morning, he was dead.

Such tragedies were needless, according to the third book of the Bible, Leviticus. Chapter 17 verse 11, written 3,500 years ago, states, "That life of the body is in the blood." God would never desire for our life-giving blood to be drained from us as a healing method. A careful reading of Leviticus reveals numerous preventative health measures given to the Israelites from the Lord through Moses. God promised his people that if they would faithfully follow him, "I will not bring on you any of the diseases I brought on the Egyptians" (Exodus 15:26). Just ponder the many diseases and infections that can be detected through a simple blood test the next time you go in for a physical. Many of them present no symptoms if caught early enough. In other words, we often don't even know that there is something wrong with us until our blood work comes back from the lab!

We love our doctors, but truth be told, the history of medicine is not pretty. Well into the nineteenth century, perhaps one-third of patients died from unnecessary infections. Many were women just having gone through childbirth. Germs had not yet been discovered, and physicians rarely washed their hands as they moved from one patient to another. At best, they would rinse their hands in a bowl of water, then reuse the *same* bowl throughout the day. Yes, I'm thankful to be living in this century. How could the Bible have helped prevent this massive suffering? In Leviticus 15:13, God instructs each person to cleanse himself "with *running* water and he will be clean." God disclosed this vital truth centuries ago!

The Black Death in fourteenth-century Europe took seventeen million lives. Healthy family members often sat in rooms with dying relatives. Later on, these same people would become ill and die themselves. What could be done? No one knew the answer. However, the Bible revealed the solution. God always wants us to be blessed with strength, good health, and longevity. So he gave us Leviticus 13:46— *quarantining*. When a human being has an infection, "he must live outside the camp." In other words, he must be separated to keep others from exposure to the same illness. These wise words could only have come from God. Moses *did* write them down, but he was raised in Egypt's royal courts, instilled with the empire's own form of medicine. Ancient records show that the prescribed cure for an infection was to apply fly dung to the wound! Ugh! Only God could have enlightened Moses after he led his people out of Egypt.

Does it make much difference what day a baby boy is circumcised? Modern science provides evidence that God wanted to help us know the correct answer four thousand years ago. He speaks to Abraham in Genesis 17:11–12, "Circumcision…will be a sign of the covenant between me and you. For the generations to come, every male among you who is *eight* days old must be circumcised." Why is the eighth day so much better than any other day? God knew why. Lab research has shown that Vitamin K reaches its peak in males on their eighth day of life. Vitamin K increases blood clotting and prevents infection. On the ninth day, its levels begin to decrease. Several medical articles have confirmed these stunning facts. God imparted to Abraham the absolutely best day for a circumcision to take place. He cares about us!

Do you remember learning about the water cycle in school? The Bible teaches it, too, in the books of Job and Ecclesiastes. Job is perhaps the Bible's oldest book, written even before Genesis. One might expect a four-thousand-year-old book to be simplistic and crude, but it is articulate and detailed. Here are its specific words concerning evaporation and condensation: "He draws up the drops of water, which distill from the mist as rain, then the clouds pour down their moisture, and abundant showers fall on mankind" (Job 36:27). That's a perfect description of our water cycle. The Bible is way ahead of its time!

While we're on the subject of water, God says the following in Job 38:16, "Have you journeyed to the springs of the sea, or walked in the recesses of the deep?" These words were mysterious until 1973 when a deep-sea research submarine expedition discovered springs of water shooting out from deep under the ocean floor. Genesis 7:11 mentions them as well, as the waters rose during the great flood: "On that day, all the springs of the great deep burst forth." So God gave us a true picture of Noah's ark and the flood by including a scientific fact not confirmed until the twentieth century—the springs of the sea!

Ancient Egyptians taught that the universe had no starting point and that it is eternal. This means it has always existed. Some religions teach the same concept even now. However, Genesis 1:1 states, "In the beginning, God *created* the heavens and the earth." It requires only one verse taken out of the entire Bible to tell us the obvious truth: the universe had a "beginning," and it was "created." All other theories in contrary start with the unstated presumption that something can come from nothing. As my former pastor used to explain it, "First, there was nothing. Then there was something." By itself, matter cannot and does not suddenly appear out of nowhere. Many ingenious articles have been written on the subject, but any rational person will reject them as outright nonsense. All matter is a creation requiring a creator. Our universe has not existed forever because Almighty God had to form it!

In the Middle Ages, astronomers thought they could count all the stars at night. One man claimed there were 1022, and the matter was settled. Years later, the number was revised downward to 965. That figure prevailed for quite a while until the new count became 1564. On and on it went. This was a fruitless effort since the Bible already held the answer 2,500 years ago. The prophet Jeremiah wrote, "For this is what the Lord says… I will make the descendants of David…as *countless* as the stars in the sky and as *measureless* as the sand on the seashore" (Jeremiah 33:22). Scientists now tell us that there are at least two trillion galaxies, each one containing millions of stars. And these are only the galaxies that have been detected! Of course, there are many more. Truly, the stars are *countless* indeed.

Are you skeptical? Do you require solid evidence before you will believe anything supernatural? Will you believe it even then, even after you are presented with the evidence? What are you holding on to? You won't lose a thing by giving God a chance in your life. You can see from these two pages that God is at least as intelligent as a lifelong skeptic. He wants to reveal himself much more to you if you will just talk to him. You can also open up a Bible, read John or the Psalms, and see what God presents. Have an open mind. Maybe you've missed something all these years. Perhaps God actually loves *you.*

The Jewish People and
God's Great Love

S ome people think that God has changed. They have the notion
that he was once angry, threatening, vengeful, demanding, and
completely unapproachable. He displayed these attributes for centuries and then flipped a switch and began to demonstrate his loving,
compassionate side when Jesus appeared on earth. In other words,
God chose to show a wrathful, condemning side throughout the Old
Testament (OT) and then his unconditional, long-suffering side in
the New Testament (NT).

Such thinking presents a confusing image of a Creator who supposedly exhibited two distinct and separate facets of his character.
For two thousand years, he presented one, and for the next two thousand, he changed to the other.

After studying the Bible, attending small group studies, and listening to sermons over the past forty years, I think I've come to a
more balanced viewpoint on this subject. Why? Simply because I've
found many verses in the OT which show God to be the same loving
Father of the NT. These scriptures are seldom highlighted and are
even overlooked so as to escape our attention. Yet they fill us with the
same powerful appreciation of God's goodness as any verse written
by the first-century apostles.

For instance, I'm overwhelmed with these words from 400 BC:
"The joy of the Lord is our strength" (Nehemiah 8:10). The Holy
Spirit touches my heart as I read Nehemiah, just as it does whenever
I peruse Jesus's similar words from the gospels: "I have told you all of

these things so that my joy may be in you and your joy may be full" (John 15:11). God was revealing his personal, relational qualities to us long before Jesus's arrival. He wants us to know his joy! Therefore, he is not a distant, brooding deity in the OT pages but an indescribable wonder who offers the deepest, one-on-one friendship to all people.

King David wrote, "Praise be to the Lord, for he showed his wonderful love to me" (Psalm 31:21). Again, I'm blown away by these precious words about our Lord's nature. This is my favorite verse in all the Psalms. How much more awesome and caring can God get? He aims that scripture right at my heart, and it hits me with full strength. If he loves me that much before Jesus was even sent to us, how much better will it become in the NT? I'm crying as I type this because I just love him back. Perhaps the Psalms are hiding some treasures meant for you as well, and you will find them by searching purposely with open eyes and heart.

"I have loved you with an everlasting love; I have drawn you with loving-kindness" (Jeremiah 31:3). This winsome verse from 600 BC sounds as if it comes right out of the NT. No doubt God was already offering his intimate, eternal love to us, if only we will listen. Yes, Jesus later fulfilled everything perfectly and tore down the barrier of sin between ourselves and the Lord. Yet I can sense the Father's heart for us, longing for us just as clearly centuries before the coming of Christ. Do you see the great kindness of God toward you in these words? Oh, he is so kind, and he always has been.

Deuteronomy is the fifth and last book of the Torah, or Law, given by the Lord to Moses. Laws are firm and direct. Their tone is stern and unrelenting. Otherwise, we would not take them seriously. So would God reveal his compassionate ways within a book of warnings and potential judgments? I say *yes*, and I find Deuteronomy to be the book of John of the OT. That may sound like a stretch, but have you ever noticed the following passages concerning his tender love and affection for the Israelites?

> For the Lord your God, who is among you,
> is a great and awesome God. (Deuteronomy
> 7:21)

He did not set his affection on you and choose you because you were more numerous than other peoples, for you were the fewest of all peoples. But it was because the Lord loved you. (Deuteronomy 7:7–8)

Yet the Lord set his affection on your forefathers and loved them, and he chose you, their descendants, above all the nations, as it is today. (Deuteronomy 10:15)

Out of all the peoples on the face of the earth, the Lord has chosen you to be his treasured possession. (Deuteronomy 14:2)

I see the same gracious Father here that I read about in John. His heart cries out for you and me, and he wants to embrace us and hold us tight.

Near the very end of Deuteronomy, after all has been said and done, this verse leaps off the page: "The eternal God is your refuge, and underneath are the everlasting arms." Wow! God is actually saying that he is extending his strong, protective arms now and forever! I receive comfort and confidence when I read this promise. It couldn't get much better. And again, I desire to love him back.

For the last several years, the words of Jeremiah 29:11–13 have become widely known. They are often quoted to reassure us in times of worry, loss, and indecision. The prophet speaks God's message, "For I know the plans I have for you, plans to prosper you and not to harm you, plans to give you hope and a future. Then you will call upon me and come and pray to me, and I will listen to you. You will seek me and find me when you search for me with all your heart." That's even worth reading twice.

No one cares about us more than God does. He is declaring that he offers a wonderful plan for our lives, and we are not alone as we look into our uncertain futures. He wants to give us "hope," and asks us to pray and to search after him because he "will listen." These solid promises are absolutely tremendous, but my favorite part appears at the end. This is not a dry exchange between God and mankind; rather, we are being urged to find the Lord's direction by seeking him "with all your heart." He desires a personal relationship with us simply because he loves every person and dearly wants us to know him. We can become close to him this very day.

Do you realize that God describes himself in detail in the book of Exodus? He allows us to comprehend his character so that there is no guesswork to be done. Here is what he says to Moses, "'The Lord, the Lord, the compassionate and gracious God, slow to anger, abounding in love and faithfulness, maintaining love to thousands and forgiving wickedness, rebellion and sin'" (Exodus 34:6–7). The first time I saw these verses, I was so awestruck that I had to review them. When God tells me he is "slow to anger," I wonder why, but at the same time, I'm extremely glad. I've turned against him many times. When I'm sorry, he extends his forgiveness and peace through his Son, Jesus, who died for me. He lets me start over.

As it turns out, God's great love for us has never changed, but his grace, through the cross, changed everything. Now I know that someday I'll be in heaven forever, and it will be my real home. Often, I can scarcely wrap my mind around someone I worship who cares about me, my faults, and my problems. I'll continue to talk to God every day. He is so worth it! I hope you'll do the same.

Yes, God loves you whether or not you like it or believe it. You can see that the Bible is filled with his amazing offers to have a relationship with you. He will pursue you because he is after your heart. Why not respond the way King David did in Psalm 18:1? With joy he said, "I love you, O Lord, my strength."

Isaiah 53 Comes True!

Isaiah 53 describes a man who is a sinless, submitted, sin-bearing, suffering, sacrificial servant and savior, substituting in our place for our own wrongdoing. That's a total of eight words which begin with the letter *s*. Alliteration is an interesting literary device, but these descriptive words are valid and worth knowing. The great prophet Isaiah was writing in 700 BC, long before this man would appear.

Who was he writing about? Some say *Israel.* Some say *Isaiah himself.* However, Israel and Isaiah were not and are not *sinless.* Israel does not *submit* to anyone. And neither one can be considered a *sin bearer.* That title can only be given to Jesus of Nazareth. He is the one person perfectly fulfilling the prophet's predictions of long ago. Isaiah didn't know who he was describing, but God evidently did.

Beginning in verse 2 (NIV), "He had no beauty or majesty to attract us to him, and nothing in his appearance that we should desire him." Because he was a leader, we tend to think of Jesus as tall and handsome. He just can't be average looking. That wouldn't work. However, perhaps good looks would have distracted many from his vital message. Maybe they would have followed him for all the wrong reasons. In any case, God's not in the business of pleasing us. The cinematic Jesus is just our own idea.

A more important theme emerges in verses 3–4. Jesus was disliked, and, like many other people, I asked incredulously, "Why?"

> He was despised and rejected by men, a man
> of sorrows and familiar with suffering. Like one
> from whom men hide their faces, he was despised

> and we esteemed him not. Surely he took up our
> infirmities and carried our sorrows, yet we con-
> sidered him stricken by God, smitten by him and
> afflicted.

"We esteemed him not" means we did not care. And "we considered him stricken by God" indicates that we thought he was being
punished on the cross for *his own* sins—not ours.

Next, we rejected him even more. "But he was pierced [nailed]
for our transgressions, he was crushed [crucified] for our iniqui-
ties; the punishment that brought us peace was upon him, and by
his wounds [stripes or whip marks] we are healed" (verse 5). God
demands payment for sin. Either we will pay or out of his great love,
Jesus pays. We cannot enter heaven unforgiven. Will we allow our
pride to cause us to reject Christ? Simply ask God to forgive you
today, and thank him for sending Jesus to save you.

Isaiah explains our situation well. Jesus "was led like a lamb to
the slaughter" (verse 7) and "we all, like sheep, have gone astray, each
of us has turned to his own way" (verse 6). "Yet it was the Lord's will
to crush (crucify) him and cause him to suffer" (verse 10). God loves
you so much that he sent his Son to die for you. I have to recognize
that fact as well. Attempting to be a *good person* falls short, and it
insults God's character. Try talking to him humbly, and forget trying
to justify yourself. He knows you.

God begins to speak, starting in verse 11, "After the suffering of
his soul, he will see the light of life and be satisfied." This scripture
proclaims the resurrection, for death is not the victor. Jesus has overcome the grave by his sinless life, his submission to his Father's will,
and his suffering for our sins on the final day of his earthly life. He
opened up heaven to anyone who would believe in him, and now we
can share in eternal life with our Savior. What an offer! Or we can
turn it down and be separated from God forever.

Then Isaiah 53 ends this way: "For he (Jesus) bore the sin of
many, and made intercession for the transgressors (mankind)" (verse
12). Since God caused the prophet to express Christ's sacrifice for
us in perfect detail, then isn't God capable of other miracles as well?

You'll find that a miracle will take place in your heart when you ask Jesus to become the Lord of your life. He will change you, and you will come to know him personally. Please accept this invitation for it's a free gift from God. He really loves you!

The Shocking Facts of Isaiah 53

S ome people prefer a cross-less Christ, a blood-free Christianity, and a feel-good gospel. They are turned off at the thought of suffering associated with religion. Pain and punishment seem quite unnecessary if we believe that Jesus's earthly role was simply to teach us to become better people. However, these are man's thoughts, not God's thoughts. To paraphrase Isaiah 55:8–9, his ways are higher than ours.

When someone is called upon to pay for every person's sins past, present, and future, that will require an unimaginable amount of pain. That's what God, our Father, asked Jesus to do—for us. Why? The reason: God cannot tolerate sin in his presence. No matter if we think we are so-called good people, we need the forgiveness of a Savior in order to enter heaven and to be declared righteous by God. If you don't agree, then you'll have to answer as to why Jesus declared, at the Last Supper, "This is my blood poured out for many for the forgiveness of sins" (Matthew 26:28). The justice and holiness of God throughout the Bible lead to our need of repentance and to his offer to pay for all our wrongs.

Jesus went through terrible treatment for you and me. A Roman whipping was greatly feared. A victim was lashed dozens of times with whips laced with lead, bone, metal, and glass. Many died or went insane before ever hanging on a cross. Jesus somehow survived the whipping, the beatings that followed, and the crown of three-inch thorns, only to be made to drag his cross uphill for the length of six football fields. From there, he had seven-inch spikes driven into his feet and five-inch spikes piercing his wrists. It's no wonder that the word *excruciating* comes from the root word *crucify*.

In 700 BC, when Isaiah wrote the word *pierced*, the punishment of crucifixion had not yet been invented. The Persians developed this method of execution four hundred years later. The prophecy was fulfilled completely. Many victims hung on crosses for days, eaten by wild dogs and pecked by birds. It was the cruelest death devised. Jesus succumbed after six hours, with his shocking physical demeanor described in detail in Isaiah 52:14: "Just as there were many who were appalled at him—his appearance was so disfigured beyond that of any man and his form marred beyond human likeness." Plus, the prophet's vision two chapters earlier adds to Christ's afflictions: "I offered my back to those who beat me, my cheeks to those who pulled out my beard; I did not hide my face from mocking and spitting" (Isaiah 50:6).

We can go through life not thinking about what happened to Jesus, but we would be avoiding God. We would be fleeing from the truth, and we know it. Standing before the Lord someday soon, all of us will have to account for our many sins. We don't tell God, "Just let me into heaven. Just forgive me." He cannot do such a thing unless someone has taken our sins away. Without our solid belief in a Savior on that day, we are left on our own. Personally, I do not wish to face God all alone. Jesus's forgiveness will allow me to join him in heaven forever. I want him by my side now and in the never-ending life to come.

Someone once said that Christianity is the only religion in the world which has, as its pivotal moment, the humiliation of its God. That's entirely true. What other religion would ever allow its god to be slapped, spit on, blindfolded, beaten, mocked, whipped, nailed, and speared? How unthinkable that would be. We will never know the full extent of Jesus's anguish, but it should have been our own suffering instead.

Is God *for* us? *Yes*, according to Jesus's own voice, "For God *loved* the world so much that *he gave* his one and *only Son*, so that whoever believes in Him will not perish (die), but will have everlasting life" (John 3:16). That is the world's favorite verse in the entire Bible by the way, and it's a good idea to ponder every single word! This one too: "No one comes to the Father except through me" (John 14:6).

Two Types of Evolution

In April 1966, *Time* magazine came out with its first-ever cover with no picture. Instead, there were only three large words: "Is God Dead?" That was pretty shocking and depressing to see. As a sixteen-year-old at the time, I wasn't aware of the questioning it took that could even lead up to such an idea.

Perhaps twenty years from now, another magazine will surprise us once again with a cover which reads, "Is Evolution Dead?" We could be heading in that direction right now. The theory of evolution (which is so often accepted as fact) has been taking more big hits from critics and authors than ever before.

First of all, people who discuss this subject rarely define their terms. It's usually a matter of "Do you believe in evolution?" Or the case is already closed: "Evolution cannot be questioned. It's been proven." Or even, "Scientists hold to evolution. Christians cling to the creation story in Genesis."

There are two kinds of evolution, however, and each one is unique. Microevolution is a fact. This refers to changes within a species. For instance, there are 360 different dog breeds, but they are still dogs. From Chihuahua to rottweiler, all dogs descended from the wolf. It's hard to believe but true.

Then there is macroevolution, and that's where the debate begins. As Charles Darwin proposed, one species can and does change into another species over time. Fish eventually become human beings, for instance. Just give it billions and billions of years and anything can happen. And people begin to think, "Yes, with enough time, it's possible." Or it's *impossible*! The grotesque-looking, transitional fossils of one species or kind becoming another haven't been found. There should be millions of them by now.

Besides, the mutational changes required for one kind to morph into another pose a huge problem. Mutations are almost always deadly. A species will die off before ever becoming another species. Evolutionists claim that slow, random activity, blind chance, and chaos lead to macroevolution. They say these processes work very gradually, but the monstrous-looking, evolving creatures they would produce could easily suffer extinction as they are enduring thousands of unbelievable body part alterations. Even given eons of time, a fish becoming a person would make a five-year-old laugh. Children are wise.

Evolutionists don't like to discuss origins anymore. Without a creator, all they are left with are rocks. That's correct: life came from rocks. They won't say that, but it's what they have to believe. What else was there before life? Just rocks. Okay, throw in a little moisture, perhaps, but that still won't produce anything viable. And since life can't even be produced in a laboratory-controlled setting these days, how could it have possibly sprung up *spontaneously* millions of years ago on its own?

Darwin is usually treated as a god. Scientists agree that he has been proven wrong about a few things, but overall, he is untouchable. Darwin believed that all life arose from a simple life form: one-celled organisms. The problem is that there's no such thing as a simple life form! Today's atomic force microscopes have revealed that even amoebas are more complex than any computer. How could *they* have evolved? If Darwin could have had access to our technology in the nineteenth century, he might have said, "Wait a minute, people. It was only a theory. Slow down. I'm not sure if I even believe it myself."

Evolutionists are stumped by males, females, and reproduction. There should be no need for two genders. Evolution, over time, seeks the most efficient route. We should be reproducing by simple cell division, called mitosis, or by some other similar means. Moreover, as husbands and wives build a family, it requires a lot of *wasted, extra* time and energy to do so. That's according to evolutionary thinking. I say it's far better and wiser to believe that the complex, specialized reproductive organs we possess were designed by a creator. That goes for all of nature as well. There was a beginning. Something did come from nothing. And only the Creator God can pull that one off.

Can We Question Evolution?

◆

Microevolution is true. Macroevolution is…well, see what you, the reader, decide. My first essay titled "Two Types of Evolution" should be read first, and this one is a follow-up.

Evolutionists sometimes take on an "of course" attitude. *Of course*, evolution is completely true. *Of course*, it's a foregone conclusion. *Of course*, it's not even worth a discussion because evolution was proven years ago. What are you doing by raising questions? *Of course*, you're already wrong.

Don't use these four words around an evolutionist: complex, intricate, specialized, or designed. They mean almost nothing, and they imply the *g word*. If you mention any of these, then the next thing out of your mouth may well be the word *god*. You are implying that a creator exists if you say those words, especially specialized or designed. Yet that's exactly what nature looks like. Animals are fully formed, high-functioning creatures. They didn't get that way by evolving; they had to be fully formed from the beginning. If not, then you get a nonfunctioning, dead organism, and no life on earth.

How would a heart ever start to beat in any living creature? It has to work well or not work at all. There can't be a step-by-step undertaking. A heart displays a specialized design. That doesn't happen through random, chaotic, blind chance evolution. You don't go from having no heart to a perfectly rhythmic heart that will beat without pause for eighty years in a human being. It has to function extremely well the first time. There are no second chances or a species will never be viable. Who starts a heart anyway?

The same pattern holds true for other body parts. Scientists who don't buy the evolution theory often point to the human eye, with its many highly complex parts. If even one part doesn't work, then eyesight fails. The chances of each of the eye's needed components functioning perfectly all at once are astronomical. Evolutionists ask you to believe that we evolved from having no eyes to high-functioning vision. It's sort of like having a pile of dirt emerge from the earth and form the highest quality camera. They say that if you allow billions of years to pass by, this natural process can, will, and has happened.

If you believe we have the primitive fossils to prove the stages of evolution, then you've been listening to the wrong scientists. Evolutionists conveniently leave out the Cambrian Period. During that long stage, thousands of creatures appeared on earth for the first time, fully formed with *no* previous fossil remains of their prior existence in primitive form. In other words, they *just appeared on the scene out of nowhere,* as if somebody made them and left a record of their fossil evidence on earth. Nothing led up to their coming—a stunning blow to evolution. No wonder this is called the *Cambrian Explosion* because many animals burst into sudden existence. Could it be possible that a creator created them?

Also, left out of most discussions are dinosaurs, which supposedly died out sixty-five million years ago. Not so fast. Within the last fifteen years, several reputable paleontologists have discovered soft, pliable tissue, including blood vessels, in dinosaur bones. You can view several videos on YouTube showing such tissue under a microscope being stretched about with tweezers. After sixty-five million years? That's not supposed to happen with *any* kind of fossil that old. The jury is still out on this astonishing, recent development.

Here's another instance in which the evolutionist has no answer. How can a male sperm and a female egg unite to form a zygote? The zygote develops into a human baby. We've all seen videos of this fusion process under magnification as the two become one. How could so much exact information be exchanged between the sperm and egg? How could an unbelievable process possibly go right the first time? If it doesn't, then we have no human race. I suspect that the Master Designer is involved. Do you? Jesus Christ confirmed the Genesis creation account in his teachings. So why not listen to him?

If Jesus Is Just a Good Man

Many people think they are being noble and magnanimous when they say, "Jesus was a good man." Some are even more generous when they allow themselves to declare that "Jesus was a good man and a great moral teacher." Others will go even further and state these words: "Jesus was a great example and an inspiration to many." They believe that they have offered up the pinnacle of well-deserved praise, fitting for a remarkable individual who changed human history forever. They would even rank Jesus among the top ten most influential figures over the past two millennia.

Is this the highest tribute that the man from Nazareth should receive? Is there more to consider when we assess him objectively? Perhaps the *good man* idea is an unfitting compliment when we actually take time to read the biblical accounts of his impactful life. Serious information awaits our discovery.

A decent, intelligent fellow worthy of respect does not walk among people and refer to himself as "the Son of God" (John 10:36). The phrase *Son of God* is not a lesser title than the word *god*. It means that Jesus is making himself equal to God and is even calling *himself* God. In addition, when he would call God "My Father" (John 10:29–30), he was again claiming deity for himself. Should we trust his words?

Another name which Jesus called himself much more often was *the Son of Man*. This is a messianic claim, taken from Daniel 7:13, prophesying the long-awaited Savior to come. Is Jesus really that person?

Jesus said to certain people, "Your sins are forgiven." The indignant religious leaders of his day thought, "Why does this fellow talk like that? He is blaspheming! Who can forgive sins but God alone?" (Mark 2:7). Jesus knew what they were thinking and rebuked them for it. Did he have the right to do so?

The book of John is filled with Jesus's "I am" statements. A good person simply doesn't speak this way. Here are a few of his claims from John's gospel:

I am the light of the world. (John 8:12)

I am the bread of life. (John 6:35)

I am the good shepherd. (John 10:11)

I am the resurrection and the life. (John 11:25)

I am the way, the truth, and the life. No one comes to the Father except through me. (John 14:6)

These are bold assertions. Should we believe him?

When many of his followers worshiped him, Jesus accepted their decisions. He did not say, "No, I'm just a good human being. Stop what you're doing."

The disciple Peter told him, "You are the Christ, the Son of the living God" (Matthew 16:16). Jesus blessed Peter for his accurate words. Is he worthy of worship?

Matthew, Mark, Luke, and John often state that Jesus "spoke with authority." Jewish leaders would teach by quoting rabbis of the past, but Jesus boldly declared, "But *I* say to you...," "Therefore *I* tell...," and "Therefore everyone who hears these words of *mine* and puts them into practice..." Chapters 5–7 of Matthew contain nine of these strong pronouncements. His words amazed the crowds.

A mere man would never say, "This is my blood poured out for you for the forgiveness of your sins" (Matthew 26:28). This quote from the Last Supper tells us that Jesus is more than a great teacher. He is willing to suffer so that God can forgive us. And he does just that—nailed to a rough cross for six hours.

John 3:16 reveals that "God loved the world so much that he gave his one and only Son, so that whoever believes in him will not perish, but will have everlasting life." When Jesus Christ rose from the dead, he proved to us that we can live eternally with him in heaven. What a rich offer! God loves you, but do you love him? Jesus was God in the flesh. We never need to call him just a good man or great man again.

The Amazing Jesus

The word *amazing* wasn't always tossed around so easily as it is in today's culture. Currently, most everything is called *amazing*. This adjective can refer to someone's hairstyle, attire, voice, lifetime achievements, athletic performances, vehicle horsepower, stylish home, mouthwatering food, or even precocious children. The word has become an all-encompassing, overly familiar term. We don't even need to come up with a synonym. *Amazing* will always do the trick.

While reading the Gospel of Mark one night, I noticed how many times *amazed* is used in relation to Jesus Christ. So I started counting, and the total number is sixteen. Since there are only sixteen chapters, that's an average of one time per chapter. Exactly what were the people in Mark so *amazed* about?

Two thousand years ago, this word meant much more. You had to be someone unique to leave a crowd completely awestruck over what they had just seen and heard. Jesus was that kind of special person. Here are some of the reasons he triggered such strong responses from the people he passionately loved.

First of all, his audience was not just a few dozen stragglers. There are over thirty verses in the New Testament referring to the large crowds that continually pressed upon him. The Gospel of Luke states that "many thousands had gathered, so that they were trampling on one another" (Luke 12:1). We might ask, "Well, if that's the case, then where are the huge numbers of faithful Christians *these* days? Where have they gone?" The answer is that they still exist but are simply more dispersed around the globe. The good news has spread near and far. Jesus now has over 2.4 billion followers worldwide.

People were *amazed* at his teachings, his miraculous healings, his absolute authority over evil spirits, and even his very words. He heals a leper, a paralytic, and a man with a shriveled hand all within Mark's first three chapters. He brings a twelve-year-old girl back to life with a command. He casts out demons four different times, restoring each person to normalcy. He heals a woman who has been bleeding for twelve years when she merely touches his robe. A blind man and a deaf mute are both cured when they encounter him. And in chapter 9, verse 15, the people are "overwhelmed with wonder" just *seeing* Jesus walking toward them! Honestly, this short book packs a wallop, bringing renewed faith and excitement to my heart as I absorb every story. Mark is so action-packed that I'm completely enthralled. Jesus is so astonishing and powerful that he compels me to choose to believe him or not. I do believe!

Interestingly, the word *amazed* is not found in the final chapter describing his resurrection. Why not? There's a good reason. This chapter dispels the notion that the first disciples were merely a gaggle of simpleminded, gullible men, for in truth, they would not easily accept the idea that a man could come back from the dead. They would need to talk and mingle with Christ several times in order to change their set thinking. When Jesus appeared to them, "he rebuked them for their lack of faith and their stubborn refusal to believe those who had seen him after he had risen" (Mark 16:14). Slowly, their doubts would disappear. In time, all the disciples would dedicate themselves and even lose their lives for the One who had defeated the curse of death forever.

Throughout history, some individuals have attempted to discredit all the miracles described in Mark and leave us only with Jesus, the popular motivational speaker—just a fellow who shared some kind, encouraging teachings. However, if his supernatural actions are removed, then we have no Jesus left at all, except for one fact: by his very existence, Jesus *himself* is a living miracle! How often does God come to earth as a man? The answer is *once* and once more to come. That's *amazing* in itself to contemplate for a moment! Then, if we will read of Christ's mighty deeds and decide to open our hearts and minds to his words, God will make himself known to us. The book of Mark is a wonderful place to discover who Jesus is and who *we* are as the people he loves.

The Greatest Man in History

I found these words online but cannot find the source. The message comes through loudly and clearly:

> He had no servants, yet they called him Master. He had no degree, yet they called him Teacher. He had no medicine, yet they called him Healer. He had no army, yet kings feared him. He won no military battles, yet he conquered the world. He committed no crime, yet they crucified him. He was buried in a tomb, yet he lives today! His name is Jesus.

Added to that is the well-known song from 1862. We've heard it so often that we don't think about the words. It seems like a child's song, but it truly isn't. The message is profound and the words are honest: "Jesus loves me! This I know, for the Bible tells me so. Little ones to him belong; they are weak, but he is strong. Yes, Jesus loves me! Yes, Jesus loves me! Yes, Jesus loves me! The Bible tells me so."

These days, we sometimes pride ourselves on being tolerant, broad-based, and eclectic when it comes to the great religions of the world. We view most of them as having good aspects, some of which we can embrace. Strong values, morals, and ethics can be taught by many different groups. We can perceive where appreciation and respect are greatly needed and well-deserved.

Yet just as we become comfortably open-minded, here comes Jesus, who says, "I am the way and the truth and the life. No one comes to the Father except through me" (John 14:6). Perhaps, we weren't quite expecting him to be so exclusive, but when we stop and realize it, nobody is his equal. He does not fit in with anyone's favorite list of great men either, for he is fully God on earth.

Only Jesus performed miracles, claimed to be God in the flesh, and rose from the dead. Only Jesus is written about in detail, seven hundred years before his birth, in Isaiah 53. Only Jesus could fulfill over three hundred prophecies scattered throughout the Old Testament when he was sent to walk among us. Only Jesus could conquer the grave and is alive forevermore.

He loves us dearly and still speaks to us today. One of my relatives once heard his voice as she was talking on the phone with my wife, Becky, about what to believe in. She started crying and said, "Jesus is *talking* to me right now, and he's telling me to listen to *everything* you are saying and to be your close friend. There is only *one* God, and it's *Jesus*."

Becky told me those exact words a few minutes later, and I immediately wrote them down. The date was May 31, 2014—a life-changing evening.

Because Jesus can communicate with us, that means he really did resurrect from the dead! He can even tell us that there is just one God, not any others, and that *he himself* is God. What a powerful message he gave my relative. What a strong proof he showed her of his existence and compassion for her. He loved her so much that he spoke to her directly. How precious can you get? That night is one to remember and cherish, for Jesus always urges us to "believe in me." He even caused her to cry.

The familiar song "Jesus Loves Me" should remind us of the truth. Jesus actually cares for us perfectly and wants us to talk easily with him each day. He will show us his love in tangible ways if we will pray and have faith in him. The greatest relationship of all time awaits us if we will reach out and trust Jesus.

Next Time You Think
You've Had a Hard Life

At times, I think of my life as having been challenging, difficult, and unfair. Most of us feel that way at certain moments. We compare ourselves with others who seem to have had it easier for reasons we don't understand. At that point, we often lose some of our belief in God's goodness because we feel excluded from his many blessings. Sometimes we cry out, "Why did my life have to be this tough? I didn't need so much grief!" Those are valid expressions of human emotion, but for a moment, let's shift the focus to someone else, just for a change. Once in a while, it's not about us.

It's safe to say that Jesus Christ was persecuted not only on the last day of his earthly existence but throughout his entire lifetime. In fact, the constant hatred actually started the day he was born and continued on for the next thirty-three years. Moreover, every minute that he lived was met with contempt in one form or another. He would never receive the acceptance and reverence he richly deserved.

The New Testament records Jesus's experiences in fine detail. Clearly, from the very beginning, King Herod wanted him dead as an infant. He would allow no future rivals. Herod ordered his soldiers to ride into Bethlehem and kill every male child under the age of two. Mary and Joseph heeded an angel's warning and fled with their son to Egypt just in time. The full story is presented in Matthew 2:13–23.

Was there ever a moment in which Satan didn't desire Jesus's allegiance? Matthew 4 and Luke 4 record the three powerful temptations in the wilderness—attempts to lure Christ into bowing to and worshiping the prince of demons. In each instance, Jesus quoted scripture to answer these unprovoked attacks. Satan wasn't through trying though. He would bide his time until future opportunities would arise.

When Jesus began his ministry at age thirty, many Pharisees, Sadducees, and members of the Sanhedrin soon rejected him. They plied him with contrived questions to set a trap. They stirred up the people to turn on him. They hardened their hearts even when Christ's miracles were performed before their eyes. Even worse, they plotted to kill him. How many of us could have withstood that kind of daily pressure?

It's a little-known fact that on Jesus's last day, he would endure six unfair trials with no sleep. One evening, the Jewish leaders arrested him and quickly held three illegal trials beginning in the middle of the night. Roman governor Pontius Pilate then tried him twice during the early morning, while also allowing King Herod a chance to interrogate him on his own. Spanning these hours, an exhausted Christ was spit on, slapped, mocked, beaten with fists, and whipped mercilessly even before the final verdict.

All the good he had done during his three years of ministry appeared to have come to nothing. His disciples abandoned him, and the jeering crowds rejected him. Further, they demanded that the jailed insurrectionist, Barabbas, be released instead of Jesus. In the end, the Savior's life was less valued than that of a convicted murderer. Ironically, he was about to die for such a person and for all of us as well.

After a short lifetime of constant hounding, stalking, and persecution, Jesus allowed men to have their way. At 9:00 a.m., they nailed him to a rough cross where he hung for six hours. He could have escaped! He could have come down from the cross. How many of us would have fled the scene that final day if we'd had the chance? I'm realizing 100 percent, including me. However, Jesus wasn't thinking of himself.

The next time I believe I've had a hard life, I'll remember the perfect man, the Son of God, my Savior, Jesus, who died and rose again for the whole human race. He told me to repent of my sins, ask God to forgive me, then follow him, serve him, help people, and look forward to heaven when I die. Because of Jesus's incredible life and the sacrifice he made, I know that God loves me. That's the joyful, good news!

Jesus Was an Extrovert

In the late twentieth century, a study of men appeared in the news. It concluded that the average man dies with two living friends. Years later, the same study was repeated, only to discover that the average male was now passing away with only one friend! My reaction was, "You mean now we're doing even worse than before? Didn't we learn anything?" And if having one friend is the *average*, then just think about the many men who must have had *no* friends at the end.

Does this seem sad to you? It does to me. Is it the best we can do? More importantly, does God want our lives to turn out that way? Many people passively withdraw from almost all personal encounters once the workday concludes. Phones, laptops, and TV take over on evenings and weekends, replacing the need for real, live human beings. We hear more voices than ever before, but we have become more isolated than ever before. We end up joining nothing, belonging to nothing, and sadly, needing almost no one. Social media and surface-level relationships give us a false sense of contentment, but we have almost forgotten the joy of eye-to-eye, lengthy, highly bonding conversations. When we are always too busy for true friendships, then we are setting ourselves up to be the eighty-year-old loners of the future. We're not thinking ahead to a frightening time when we will become too set in our ways to change.

Here's a good example of a proactive man with an intentional agenda. Even if he had owned a tablet, a DVR, and wireless earbuds, he would have set them aside and put people first. Jesus extended himself to individuals—to all sorts of men and women. He was highly relational in his daily interactions, as he went about teaching, healing, listening, sharing meals, and giving of himself to the point of deep fatigue. He traveled with twelve men for three years, leading them toward full discipleship. For all his efforts, he was derisively called "a glutton and a drunkard, a friend of tax collectors and 'sinners'" (Matthew 11:19).

Jesus was the extrovert we would do well to emulate. We can't become just like him, but we can strive to leave our shells and realize that people will blossom from our friendship. We seldom think that way. It's usually a case of "What do *I* want? What can *I* get out of this endeavor?" Basically, that means "What's in it for me?" However, we rarely put the shoe on the other foot and ask, "Who needs me? Who could really use a friend?" And maybe, "Why am I becoming so shy and reclusive that I can't get over myself?"

Jesus understood that people needed him desperately. They need us too! Yes, people long for a friend like you and me, usually without knowing it. They will benefit from our godly influence, our faithfulness, our encouraging words, and our uplifting demeanor. As Christians, the Lord has given us those gifts to share. It's a sin to keep them to ourselves, for the Bible plainly tells us not to commit sins of omission. This means that when we understand the right thing to do and we don't do it, we fail God.

In Luke, Jesus spotted the short local Jewish tax collector Zacchaeus up in a tree. As he passed by, Jesus said to him, "Zacchaeus, come down immediately. I must stay at your house today" (Luke 19:5). Talk about being extroverted! Jesus began to form a relationship with this hated man, resulting in his desire to repay all the people whom he had cheated out of their money. Christ could have walked right past this fellow, as we would have done, and no one but God would have cared. But *Jesus cared!*

When was the last time that we called up an imperfect person whom we know in order to have a good talk? Or asked such a person out to lunch? Or invited him or her to our homes? Jesus would have done that if he had *had* a home. He did the next best thing though—he extended himself so far that he even invited *himself* to *their* homes. Aren't we glad he did this? Do we love people as much as he did? I'm working on it. I've been blessed with several close friends. More importantly, they have my friendship as well! We are greatly needed, more so than we allow ourselves to realize. Imitating Jesus is the right decision. Why should our lifestyle be 180 degrees different from his lifestyle? That's a question worth asking God.

Good Reasons Not to Read the Bible

People have many reasons why they avoid the Bible. Here are a few that I've heard. Correct that: here are all the objections that I've uttered over the years. By grouping them together, it sounds like this: "It's boring. It's old. It's too long. I'd rather do something more exciting. I already know what it says. It's so repetitious. I've heard all the stories before. I can't understand it. Too many *thees* and *thous.* Nobody reads it anymore. I had too much of it growing up. It makes me feel judged. Just be a good person. I don't like to read books. How do you know it's true, anyway? I don't know where to begin."

These are very strong and sincere objections. Yet I love to read the Bible nowadays. I often put it off until late at night, but a day without it leaves me feeling sad, incomplete, and stuck in the material world. The good reasons to avoid the book turned into great reasons to delve into it. I'm seventy-two now, but the Bible seemed like a foreign object for several years. So what caused me to change slowly and steadily?

The King James Version contains all the archaic language. Many people still use it, but I've said my goodbyes. The modern language New International Version was becoming very popular just when I needed direction in my late twenties. Friends told me about it, so I bought my own copy and could see the difference right away. It presented the Bible in an easy-to-read, beautiful style. Suddenly, this bulky book was coming alive for me. I had read parts of it as a teenager, then cast it aside in college, and had almost forgotten all that I learned. Now I was starting to recall this great man, Jesus, whom I had once admired.

Where to start? Matthew, Mark, Luke, and John will describe everything you never knew that you didn't know about a Savior who loves you. He wants you to seek him, and you'll never be the same if you do. The book of John got to me immediately and so did Mark. Mark displays a concise, fast-paced storyline while John will convince you of God's deep, everlasting care and concern for your life.

These four books, called the Gospels, aren't too long. Sometimes I wish they were longer, so I could learn even more about Jesus's uniqueness, his miracles, his sacrificial love, and his desire for me to know him. If you never met anybody who reads the Bible, ask yourself, "Who am I hanging with?" Millions of people worldwide love this book. I never began to meet them, though, until I gave the Bible a chance.

Boring, old, lengthy, and repetitious? That's what I used to think and still do if I leave it on the shelf, collecting dust. It's only then that the Bible seems useless—when I don't touch it. However, when I make an intentional decision to open it to the parts that have spoken to me, then God becomes real to my heart again. I can tell that his Holy Spirit is drawing me. God reaches my mind, as well, because his powerful words invite me to accept his wonderful Son, Jesus Christ. You will have the same opportunity.

God doesn't want to ruin all the excitement of being alive. I get to start out each morning being joyful instead of empty. In fact, most days seem to have an adrenaline high to them, all because of God's presence in my life. It's definitely exhilarating to worship and to serve my Lord. I'm not kidding!

How can you know if this book is true? There are no *Lone Ranger* Christians. If you read the Bible a bit, then ask God for a friendly, Bible-believing church. You'll need other believers for strength and wisdom. The pastor will care about your questions and will talk with you at length. Simply ask him for guidance. It's awesome to begin an intimate, personal relationship with the God who created us. Take the chance of a lifetime and grow closer to your heavenly Father who will never leave you. We need him every day.

You Can Be Sure

If someone you completely trusted promised you everlasting life, would you believe that person? If that individual came from the place of eternal life itself, would that make a difference? Yes, I'd believe such a promise from such a source. In fact, I'd be silly not to agree and to be possibly left out. That would be the mistake of a lifetime—and of my future life. I'd be not only *silly* but stupid and foolish as well.

Many people say, "Oh, I hope I'm going to heaven" or "Maybe I'm going to heaven" or even "I think I'm going to heaven." Some of them have been attending a house of worship for their entire lives, and this is the best that they can propose. Everlasting life is really just a possibility, even after having many years to think about it. However, what if this abovementioned person, who is none other than Jesus Christ, states in his own words that we can live forever? Surely, that changes everything—if we listen.

We take in more voices on a daily basis than ever before. Social media has hooked most of us, and if that's not enough, we have big-screen TVs, with awesome sound, to come home to. So just when we'd like to relax and have it quiet, we don't. Soon, we miss all the voices, anyway. We leave so little room for God, if he's there, to say anything at all. In our own little worlds, we're not poised to listen for him at any point. Yet he who knows us best greatly desires for us to know him intimately. He is very patient.

God will wait until we're ready. That might require a long time, but he will persist. In fact, he has already told us what he wants to say in the amazing teachings of Jesus. The disciple John often quoted Christ's words:

> He who believes in me, though he dies, yet shall he live. (John 11:25)

> My sheep hear my voice and they follow me. I give them eternal life, and they will never perish. (John 10:27–28)

Best of all, Jesus explained the whole reason for his coming to this earth, "God loved the world so much that he gave his one and only Son, so that whoever believes in Him will not perish, but will have everlasting life" (John 3:16). God could not have made it more evident to us that *he* is the source of all life, and we should trust and accept him. No one else can do it for us. This is called *grace*, and it's a gift we can't earn, even with our best efforts. First of all, though, we have to come clean before our Creator.

Please ask God to forgive you for all your wrongdoing and believe that Jesus bled and died to pay for your sins so that you *can* go to heaven. God is holy and desires to forgive anyone who will place his/her faith in his Son—not Jesus the good man or the great teacher or the strong founder of a major religion. No, this is Jesus Christ who imparted several compelling truths at the Last Supper. With the cup in his hand, he spoke directly to every person's conscience, "This is my blood, poured out for many for the forgiveness of sins" (Matthew 26:28). The following day, he *did* suffer immensely, died, and soon resurrected, promising he would "go and prepare a place for you there (heaven)" (John 14:2). That's the good news!

John went on to declare, "I write these things to you who believe in the name of the Son of God so that you may KNOW that you have eternal life" (1 John 5:13). Did you catch that? No longer does anyone have to wonder or guess or say "I'm not sure" about the future. God is trying to get through to our doubting minds that we can be certain that there *is* a heaven. We can enter it only by humbling ourselves before God and repenting of our sins. When the Lord forgives us through his grace, that's when we will live forever in his presence. He's a compassionate and loving God, so love him back with all you've got. He will send the Holy Spirit into your heart to comfort you. The innocent, perfect man Jesus did not die in vain. He gave up his *own* life so that you and I can experience *never-ending* life!

Facets of God's Character

From the Bible, we discover that God is great, mighty, holy, righteous, just, loving, forgiving, strong, jealous, compassionate, gracious, faithful, merciful, wrathful, everlasting, sovereign, trustworthy, wise, truthful, good, kind, patient, knowable, relational, omniscient, omnipresent, and omnipotent.

God is our Father, Creator, shepherd, strength, rock, fortress, refuge, deliverer, defender, guide, helper, healer, comforter, hiding place, hope, shelter, redeemer, salvation, provider, protector, and friend.

We are to love, adore, praise, worship, glorify, honor, exalt, thank, ask, seek, serve, obey, follow, meditate on, lift up, listen to, sing to, pray to, trust in, believe in, rest in, rejoice in, and cry out to God.

Jesus is the Savior, the Son of God, the Word, the lion, the Lamb, the good shepherd, the light of the world, the bread of life, the way, the truth, the life, the true vine, the gate, the King of kings, the Prince of Peace, the wonderful counselor, the suffering servant, and the resurrection and the life!

When we repent of our sins, we then become new creations: born again, saved, cleansed, forgiven, justified, reconciled, redeemed, and delivered.

These attributes of the Almighty are awe-inspiring but hardly exhaustive. The Bible presents so many more. What about the heart of God? We hardly ever use the term *heart* in daily life except, perhaps, when writing a card on Valentine's Day! Yet the Bible often emphasizes this precious word. Believing in God is not meant to be a dry, intellectual decision. It's more than just an acceptance. God desires for our hearts to respond to his passionate love for us. His personal relationship with those who trust in him will change our hearts forever. His great love will deeply move us as we receive the Holy Spirit.

Here are several joyful verses about our Lord, who affectionately pursues us throughout our entire lives:

> Love the Lord your God with all your heart, and with all your soul and with all your strength. (Deuteronomy 6:5)

> Trust in the Lord with all your heart. (Proverbs 3:5)

> The eyes of the Lord range throughout the earth to strengthen those whose hearts are fully committed to him. (2 Chronicles 16:9)

> You will seek me and find me when you search for me with all your heart. (Jeremiah 29:13)

> God has poured out his love into our hearts through the Holy Spirit, whom he has given us. (Romans 5:5).

The last scripture is powerful, for it promises that God will "pour out his love into our hearts." Since his desire is to bless us, we'd be silly not to take him at his word. Why would we want to miss out?

Are you the sort of person who is waiting for God to perform a miracle in front of your eyes and *then* you will admit that he's real? A miracle is a onetime event. If you saw one, then you might go the next twenty years without seeing another. What if the best miracle of all is to know God, to be close to him, and to enjoy his presence every day? I'd say reach out to him and go for the long-term relationship instead. This will require a large dose of humility, for we are separated from God through pride. Most of us don't want to hear a thing about the man who suffered on a cross so that we can receive forgiveness. Yet Jesus is our answer. He cares about you whether you know it or not. Start with, "Jesus, I do need you."

If you are a believer who has become distant from God, then look over the facets of his character to be reminded of how truly awesome he is! We forget so easily. Something on that list will stir you and bring a strong response. All it takes is an honest prayer to reconnect with the One who loves you perfectly.

Listing My Sins

Perhaps one of the rarest things a person will ever do is to take a pen and write a list of his or her sins. When I got the idea a few months ago, I was soon surprised I wrote so much! I quickly hid the paper in a drawer, not wanting anyone to see it. Finally, a few weeks later, I placed it on my dresser to remind myself what I had written. Now I'm ready to share my words, although they might offend a few readers.

I've always had this thought that when we let people know we are Christians, they often want to prove to us how good *they* are. Why is that? It could be that they think we are better people than they've been, and they feel slightly ashamed about having been far from God. Or they might think that we seem *too* good for them. Regardless, if they feel uncomfortable around Christians from the start, it can inhibit them from giving God a chance. We need to become more real about ourselves to unbelievers.

Some of us have compelling testimonies to share of deliverance from being lost, and people will listen and then say, "Wow!"

However, most Christian conversions lack deep drama, leading skeptics to ask us, "So what made you feel you were so bad? What did you actually do wrong? You seem as though you have probably tried to be a decent person your whole life."

That's why I felt an urge to write my list! It's all right if we become upfront as to how serious our sins truly are. Our openness could help someone.

My sins are *hatred, anger, envy, greed, pride, vengeance, selfishness, lying, lusting, being unforgiving, putting God last, swearing in his name, and driving through red lights.* I'll come back to that last one in a minute, but are you surprised? Well, *I am!* There are so many. Would your list be shorter? I hope so.

Some friends would say to me "Don't be so hard on yourself" or "Everybody's done those things, or at least thought of them" or "But look at all the good you've done in your life. That's what really counts."

At times, I'm tempted to believe those lines; but, in truth, I stand guilty before God. Only someone who pays for my sins can help me. Only the sinless one will do. Only Jesus would be willing to suffer greatly for all the suffering that I've caused. The ripple effect of sin is a fact which we often disregard or ignore.

Some would advise me, "Whatever you do, Charlie, don't drive through red lights." In other words, that wrong receives the most attention. That one stands out as the sin that can definitely hurt others the most, even causing death. Yet is this actually the case? According to Jesus's words, the rest of my sins bring on death and destruction as well. Sin is sin, and it offends God in every aspect because he is holy and just. By the way, I only drive through *green* lights, but see, I was lying to make a point! Not good.

I'm beginning to speak to my non-Christian friends about my long list. I hand it to them then ask them to read it out loud. I pray that they will discover two things: I'm not better than they are, and they have plenty of sins to confess too. At least, they start to think. Time will tell if this new approach bears fruit.

In the New Testament, no one ever received Christ without repenting. Still, I know people who want to embrace Jesus's teachings without any soul-searching, humility, or acceptance of the reality of a bloody cross. Much of Christianity repulses them, yet they like Jesus a great deal. That won't work! Scripture declares in 1 John 1:8, 10, "If we claim to be without sin, we deceive ourselves, and the truth is not in us… If we claim we have not sinned, we make God out to be a liar, and his word has no place in our lives." Therefore, if I talk about my sins more honestly, perhaps I can help my friends begin to see their own need for a Savior. My goal is not to shock everyone, but neither is it to cover up who I really am.

Avoiding God'sName

Do you ever notice that some of your friends or relatives never say the word *god*? *You* might say it, but they will not reciprocate. This can almost seem like a one-man contest to see how long they can go without mentioning God, even in passing. It becomes a depressing victory for them in the end. If you have never noticed this omission, maybe it's a good thing. That way you surely will have been less perplexed and incredulous than I have become with people.

In such situations, I often ask myself, "What is so great about being so careful not to speak God's name? What do you gain? How does that help anyone?" I've even known *Christians* in my own family who had unanimously resolved to discuss only subjects which did not involve the Almighty. If some aspect of one's beliefs were to come up in a conversation, it would die a quick death due to sudden tension and lack of response. I would observe cringing and jangled nerves. From Christians! I always thought that we are the ones who were meant to keep God's name alive. If we *don't,* nonbelievers certainly *won't.*

When I was taking my first psychology class (my minor) in college, I learned about positive and negative reinforcement. We all identify with the positive. That word can imply some *cheerleading*: "Good job." "Nice work." "You're doing super!" "Great game!" "Way to go!" "You rock!" "I like your text." The negative side, however, need not involve any words at all. Silence is a great technique to stop a subject from sparking a lively discussion. Most of us don't know how to deal with a silent reaction. We usually feel uneasy, and then we just give up, not wanting to add further embarrassment.

It takes determination, relentlessness, risk, and a deliberate mind-set not to let the silent responders win. Otherwise, they will gladly keep on winning. If they never verbalize God's holy name, then we can plant some spiritual seeds with varied approaches. I look for opportunities to work things into a conversation in a natural way. I might say "Thank God" or "God bless you" or "I'll pray for you." Sometimes I'll mention my church, my Bible study, or a Christian movie playing locally. I don't *dwell* on any of these. It's a quick hit; a thought instilled, perhaps. It's a way of telling others, "Here I am. This is me. This is my life. This is how I speak, even if it's different from you. And this is what I will always be like." I don't overdo it, and I also take plenty of time to discuss other topics, as well, in order to build strong relationships. Among believers, this method was once called *friendship evangelism* or *earning the right to be heard.* I agree with those concepts, but only somewhat, for if I *always* wait until I form a deep friendship, I might wind up rarely speaking about my faith at all. I greatly enjoy bantering and getting to know many people, but why pretend to be something I'm not by leaving out a subject so meaningful in my life as my beliefs? I feel empty inside if I continually fail to share my love for the Lord.

People can start to loosen up. It may take a long time, but suddenly, they begin to talk and sound like curious inquirers! I've seen it happen. So just hang in there with friends and relatives. Speak naturally and briefly about anything Christian. Let them know that you won't be suppressed. Neither will you be a pushy fanatic. (Even Christians don't care for such believers.) Keep the doors open and try not to become frustrated. It's difficult—no doubt about it. Above all, don't get angry and then stop praying for the stubborn ones.

Lift them up to God even when you can barely hope they will ever accept Christ. Your contacts can become quite interested in spiritual matters right out of the blue. Prepare for those moments because you don't want to be caught off guard or dumbfounded or *silent yourself* when they start to show some interest in your faith. You may have to wait patiently for years, but patience is a "fruit of the Spirit" (Galatians 5:22). It's the number one attribute we need when dealing with *God-avoiders.* Take heart, for the Lord can surprise us by reaching them and even changing them when we least expect it!

Who Needs a Testimony?

Do we need to have a testimony? Is it a requirement at some point? I'm not certain, but let's explore the idea. Think of a testimony as a before-and-after story. You were once this way, and now you're another way. God entered into a tough situation in which you were involved and turned it around. This might have entailed a supernatural event or simply a dramatic change of heart. God could have saved you from going down the wrong road for the rest of your years. Unexpectedly, he redirected your path.

More often, a testimony means that you were once a nonbeliever, having no use for God in your life. Then the Lord suddenly intervened, perhaps through a onetime action, causing you to become a follower of Jesus Christ. You were saved from despair only by the power of God. Had he not stepped in, you would have been lost in every sense of the word. Truth be told, God rescued you from yourself.

Yet, there's a question remaining. What if you grew up in the church since infancy? What if you were a cradle Catholic or a cradle Protestant? And what if you feel as though you have *always* believed in God and cannot remember a time when you actually accepted Christ and it changed you? You have kept only one mindset for your entire spiritual life, and nothing new has ever come along. You're a faithful Christian; you always have been and that settles it. There's no need for any second thoughts.

Some people do seem to be straight arrows. They've never veered to the right or to the left. They appear to be consistent, decent, hardworking, churchgoing, family-oriented people who would give you the shirt off their backs if needed. At first glance, an observer might declare, "Don't bother them. They're doing fine." On the other hand, could they have missed out on something quite important?

Contradicting the group consensus of what makes a *good person*, Jesus strongly asserts that "no one is good—except God alone" (Mark 10:18). Paul further states, "All of us fall short of the glory of God" (Romans 3:23). I believe that this stark news about who we really are should prompt us at least to ask ourselves if we have a testimony to share. Have we ever had an encounter with God that truly altered us? Were we ever desperate, humbled, or remorseful? Can we remember a turning point moment?

God is in the business of allowing us to really experience him. He's a relational, personal, loving Father who wants us to draw close. He has intervened, unexpectedly, many times in my own life to lead me, shield me, rescue me, and cause me to be "born again" (John 3:3). His miracles total up to about twenty-five, and I've shared a few in the past. Even so, here's the biggest one of them all: I'm not a good person. I can fool others into thinking that I am, but deep down, despite appearances, I was once lost in every way. I sought God's help. I needed his power to overtake me, overwhelm me, and change me into a "new creation" (2 Corinthians 5:17). The Lord was kind and gracious enough to do exactly that when I was a young teenager.

Years later, though, I turned into an angry, fear-ridden, sinful man in my twenties and thirties, unable to change. Only when I became broken and repentant did he enter my life again and forgave me. I'm not perfect, but I'm definitely not what I was or could have remained. God has placed his Spirit (his presence) in my heart. Peace, joy, gratitude, and praise are now my new strengths.

That's my *before-and-after* story in a nutshell. Do you have one? Do you need to talk straight to God in your own words? Don't use a memorized prayer. Speak to God using your own thoughts from deep within you. He's not a distant, detached entity. Your heavenly Father desires for you to seek him, love him, cry out to him, and find him. Lost but found! That's a real testimony we can all share together.

You Have Ten Seconds

Most people I have encountered will allow you approximately ten seconds to share the gospel. After that time allotment, they will change the subject, start to walk away slowly, or simply exhibit dead silence. These typical responses will disappoint and depress me unless I remember one thing: I have planted a seed. Someday, another person or the Lord himself will water that seed and cause it to grow.

If I could talk a blue streak, if I could browbeat, if my voice were louder or quicker, or even if I were more winsome, I might be able to hold a listener's attention much longer. However, God seems to have given me the gift of politeness and the desire to save a relationship at all costs. I can speak firmly and directly, but I always have the long-range plan in the back of my mind. That plan includes the strong possibility that there will be another day for witnessing a second time, especially to friends and neighbors. I will patiently, prayerfully wait for that second opportunity in which I'll share the good news once again. It will come along because God will time it perfectly. He will use me if I'm ready and watchful. Meanwhile, I often plan ahead and rehearse what I'm going to say.

Even with a short, ten-second witness, I still ask myself, "Did I say the right things, did I say too much, or too little, or will the person ever remember what I actually *said*?" However, I need not worry about my presentation. The other day in church, a speaker paraphrased Charles Spurgeon. I took the words to heart, quickly writing them down as best as I could: "The Word of God is like a lion. You don't have to defend a lion. All you have to do is let the lion loose, and the lion will defend itself." That image of a fierce lion running freely and silencing the critics will always stick with me now. I needed a strong mental picture to help embolden me, and Spurgeon's message really hit home.

Last week, I asked a good friend on my street, "Do you think you are going to go to heaven?"

He answered, "I don't know. I don't know."

Knowing him well, that's what I thought he would say. So I explained how to get to heaven, and he then changed the subject, as I thought he would. At least I got to speak for ten seconds a couple of times and keep our friendship alive. I'll bring up the gospel again, and I'll pray for him even more often. If it takes several years, I'll keep sharing the Word, bit by bit.

Just this month, my seventy-nine-year-old sister joined two Zoom Bible studies for the first time in her life. Did I bring that about? I had tried every angle with her since the 1980s. But no, God changed her, and he was kind enough to let me serve him along the way. Relatives are different—we can often talk far into the evening with them about spiritual matters and be much more emphatic. Yet in the end, only the Lord will make the difference. Incredibly, he is now altering the belief system of a senior citizen, which is something quite rare.

You might be saying to yourself, "Charlie, you should be able to talk for more than ten seconds with most people." Sometimes that's true. The problem is that I'm a friendly, relational, outgoing, nice guy, who is always eager to listen and learn from others. I find people fascinating, and I will stand still talking with them for long stretches. I ask many questions simply because I'm so curious about God's greatest creation: human beings. I never want to put stress on relationships, so my witnessing often comes in short sound bites. If I can save a friendship so that I'll be able to share Jesus again another day, I'll always do it. I deal with a lot of hardened hearts, and believe me, ten seconds is often all that I get. If you can do better, then go for it! I'll be cheering for you!

One Week to Live

A Christian's life is fairly easy inside the USA. Here, we are not part of the persecuted church, which we observe in many other nations. We are free to own Bibles, worship without risk, and witness as much as we want. Yes, there are ongoing court battles, but for now, we should thank God we are still able to speak in the name of Jesus Christ. We do have to wrestle with the fear of disapproval. At the same time, millions of committed believers risk torture and death on a daily basis just for possessing a Bible. Pew Research Center now declares that Christians are the most persecuted people in the entire world.

With that mental picture in mind, sometimes I ask myself, "What would I do with my time if I knew for certain I only had one more week to live?" I don't pose that problem because I'm longing for a morbid experience but only to provide clarity. The next few questions I then confront are these: "What would I do to serve God during that last week? How would I spend those final days as a Christian living in California? Do nothing different or do a whole lot more? Nearing the end, would I become like the bold witnesses we've always heard about? Or would I act with timidity even on my very last day?"

If I actually had seven days to go, I want to think that I'd phone, text, or email all my contacts about salvation through our Lord. I'd even reach out to my neighbors, relatives, and even those I hadn't been in touch with for years. I'd share the gospel directly and completely, not leaving anything out this time. No more seed planting but the full presentation—pleading and exhorting with the undecided ones to believe and receive Jesus. And if anybody were to get mad at me, how would that possibly seem intimidating? I'd have nothing to fear really. How could anyone hurt me? I'm going to die anyway! In addition, most of the small, ridiculous things that I currently worry about would just fly out the window.

Perhaps you, the reader, are asking yourself at this moment what you would do for God if you knew you only had a week left. Maybe you would react this way: "I'm doing the best I can right now. I don't see a need to change anything simply because I'm about to pass on." That's a fair answer and worthy of respect. For many Christians, though, including me, so much gladness and desire well up inside of us to share the gospel that the thought of losing *all* our trepidation would make us incredibly joyful! That's the greatest moment for a Christian—to have nothing to lose and everything to gain for Christ.

Becoming more courageous as we get closer to the end brings on another question to be faced: why wait until then? If losing our inhibitions about witnessing can take place with a few days remaining, we could ask, "What's holding us back presently?" There must be someone or something that we fear so strongly, causing us to be reluctant. Let me list a few ideas, and they probably all apply to me: my image, my reputation, scorn, ridicule, rejection, loss of friendships, looking like a fool, perceived as an annoyance, being the only Jesus follower, and going against the norm. Yes, that's me many times. Fear wins—yet, not always. For us, as believers, what God has placed in our hearts can't be held back all day long. Quite often, we are just about to burst with the good news, and then it simply spills out, touching many lives. At least, that's how my heart responds. God has filled us with his Holy Spirit, making this verse come alive: "The joy of the Lord is your strength" (Nehemiah 8:10). What an inspiring bit of truth!

I'm not saying that anyone should actually dwell on living just one more week. It does help *me* to grow when I contemplate such what-if scenarios, but I might be the only one. On the other hand, Christians know full well that worldly life is short, and eternal life is long. Therefore, heaven is more important than earth. Let's continue to tell people about our glorious Savior and where he waits for us. There's no time like the present to be sharing God's mighty message of salvation in every possible way.

What I Know for Certain

My heart always longed for a God I could talk to—a personal God. Thankfully, God turned out to be that kind of God. I didn't invent him. I didn't just hope that he would be personal and relational and then form him in my mind. No, not at all. God simply turned out to be the one who would meet my heart's deepest longings. He met *all* my needs, which is no surprise since he also created my desire for his love in the first place. I didn't dream him up nor did I imagine his existence through wishful thinking. He actually revealed himself to be the wonderful God that I wanted all along. Why would I decide to search for anything less than a close relationship with the living God? Why would anyone for that matter?

How do I know that he's real? How can I tell for sure? I will gladly declare that he put a tremendous joy in my heart that I can't create for myself. It's a supernatural joy, and it's there every day for me to experience. It's from the Holy Spirit, which Jesus promised he would send after his resurrection. Well, he sent it all right, because I'm filled with the Spirit whenever I turn to God. This is not the same as being a happy person. I don't want to settle for that because happiness is an emotion which fluctuates wildly. I'm not always happy, but the steady Holy Spirit places me in God's presence with its surpassing peace. Happiness is a fickle friend, but when God lives in me, I know his holiness, comfort, and joy—not my own.

I pick up the Bible and read actual quotes from Jesus or the passionate words of the Psalms, and God's joy begins to plant itself in my soul. The Bible comes alive and so do I! The Holy Spirit has touched me once again. I don't open the book hoping it will make me feel warm and fuzzy. This is not mind over matter. This is actually the Lord changing my dull human heart into one that he can enter with his love. Who wants a dead, serious, hardened heart for his whole life? That would be a poor choice indeed. God will soften me and make me his own if I will allow him. This can happen each day if I trust in *him* instead of in my own efforts. When I choose Jesus, a new life opens up for me, and I become a new creation.

Sometimes, after I close my Bible, I burst into spontaneous singing. Worship songs, praise songs, and even hymns flow out through my voice with no conscious decision to begin. Many minutes go by while I loudly proclaim God's goodness through the words. Once again, the Holy Spirit has overwhelmed me with rejoicing and gladness. I could keep on singing forever it seems. Did I work myself into an altered state of mind? Did I focus so intently on God that I reached hysteria? No and no again. This is the same presence of the Lord dwelling in me that Jesus promised would come to his disciples. His own words in John chapters 14–17 give us absolute assurance that God will always draw near to us if we will believe.

I greatly desire to share the gospel or to pray for the people I walk past. Do they know the Lord? Have they heard the full story of Jesus? Did they reject him already, or do they simply need another chance? Perhaps they heard a partial gospel presented unlovingly at the wrong time. Here is the public, always surrounding me every day, and all I need to do is simply open my mouth. I'm excited and scared at the same time. This is not narrow-mindedness, Bible thumping, or brainwashing. Witnessing means sharing my personal testimony or the path to salvation, which individuals can accept or reject.

God's love compels me and leads me toward those who are open. His perfect timing amazes me time and again. Can't we ever present something *new* to anyone? That's all the gospel is—good *news*. I will not be loud, forceful, argumentative, or angry. Jesus's message starts as an invitation of love from our heavenly Father to come to him freely. If I do not speak with God's love from my heart, then my witnessing will fall flat and never recover. After all, John 3:16 starts with, "God so *loved* the world…" Adding to that great verse is a saying that comes from man's wisdom: "People will never care how much you know, until they know how much you care."

How can I show that I really do care about nonbelievers? More and more often, I ask them, "Is there anything you'd like me to pray about?" Now, if somebody were to ask *me* that question, I'd be stunned and caught off guard. I would be so befuddled that any human being would actually show such an interest in me that I would automatically try to respond positively. And even if I did say "No," I'd still walk away in a state of wonder that someone could care so much and take such a loving risk in approaching me. That's exactly what happens whenever *I* ask the question. It disarms people and creates a bonding, as well as a possible relationship. I get to learn about their greatest hurts and concerns. Plus, I'm no longer viewed as the pushy believer—at least for the moment! No one is offended because, after all, to pray means to talk to God. Who would ever openly say a bad word about prayer? That would be almost unpatriotic in a sense. At the very least, it gets people thinking, "Oh yeah, prayer. It really *is* kind of important, isn't it?"

I don't walk around every minute feeling closely connected to God. With my human nature, I become prideful, thoughtless, self-centered, angry, and irritable, just like everybody. I could choose to call myself a failure. Yet I know what is certain about God because he has revealed himself to me through his Son, Jesus. I respond that I want to know him. This is not weakness but real strength. I confess that I sin and that Jesus suffered to pay for my many wrongs. He loved me that much. Should I decide that God's Son died for nothing? That would be my worst mistake to think such a lie. I *need* Jesus in my life, as does everyone else. He forgave me from the cross, reconciling me to God forevermore! I'm so grateful.

Will you believe the truth that you need a Savior too? The Bible warns us not to harden our hearts. I've been there, done that. So say a prayer to receive the Lord, and he will come into your life this very day. God will listen because he cares for you. Here's a way that you could pray, or you could simply express it in your own words:

Dear God,

I've been so far from you. I've put you last in my life for a long time. But I believe that you are calling to me, and I'm sorry that I've left you out. I've also done things that aren't very good, and when I think of Jesus's life, I know I don't measure up. Please forgive me. I want to believe in your Son. I want to follow Jesus. I need you in my life, Lord. I would like to study your word, go to a good church, and be around Christians who will be there for me. I want to leave a lot of my old life behind because it was so worldly and ungodly. I see it now. I want to turn from my past ways and become a new creation, as you promise I can be. Help me to follow you, God. I trust you will lead me wherever you want me to go. I give you my life and my heart because I really love you dearly. Thank you, Father, that Jesus suffered and died just so I would become your child and someday go to heaven. How could you love me that much? I love you, too, Lord. Thank you for coming into my heart today. Amen.

Okay, I cried as I typed that prayer. It was as though *I* was being saved all over again. But I hope it was *you*. Perhaps you are desiring to know God. Humble yourself, won't you, and give your heart to Jesus. You will never regret it. Let him change your life right now. He cares for you more than anyone could!

Grace Is More than a Prayer
at the Dinner Table

Grace indicates that we can't make it to heaven on our own. If we could, then Jesus Christ would have stayed home in heaven or could have come down to live a hundred years while teaching many more disciples. Even so, some of us feel we deserve everlasting life because we are *good people*. All right, but what if we're not good enough? And where do we find that type of belief taught by any religion?

In Hinduism and Buddhism, we would have to go through millions of reincarnations before even having a chance of reaching Nirvana, which means *nothingness*. Reincarnation is a great weight to bear, not a fun, exciting adventure to anticipate. Some Americans who dabble in this belief gleefully spout, "Oh I can't wait to see what my next life will be like." Not to Hindus. In fact, their eyes sometimes open wide whenever they are told that the Bible declares they actually only have to live one life before entering heaven. This revelation lifts the endless burden of continual rebirths off their backs and puts joy in their hearts. No longer do they have to work their way up the ladder, always uncertain if they are found worthy to move on to a higher level, even after millions of lifetimes.

Muslims believe that you can earn your way to heaven. There's an angel over your right shoulder continually writing down your good deeds and another angel over your left shoulder always recording your bad actions. This is a works-based approach. At the end of your life, they total them up, and if you're 50.1 percent good, then away you go to an afterlife filled with sensuous, worldly pleasures.

Here's a question: should we think that God is really a good deed counter? Not sure? Then what *does* cause God to pronounce us acceptable enough to enter into eternal life? Does he simply decide that we qualify because we're better than so many other people? And is that our own idea or his idea? Chances are it's our own notion, and a vague one at that. All it amounts to is a feeling which we want to cling to, hoping we will somehow merit favor based upon performance—very similar to pleasing the boss at our jobs. This is known as *making it up as we go along*. If we are realistic, however, then this kind of wishful thinking should appall us. At death, we could end up being totally wrong, and deep down, we know it.

There's another way, so perhaps we should listen to the only person who actually *came down* from heaven to save mankind. Jesus declared many times that God sent him. He preached the gospel, which means the *good news*. He *is* the gospel! No other religious figure ever appeared with such a promising message, so Jesus rightfully deserves our full attention. He said, "For my Father's will is that everyone who looks to the Son and believes in him shall have eternal life, and I will raise him up at the last day" (John 6:40). He proclaimed, "I tell you the truth, whoever hears my words and believes him who sent me has eternal life and will not be condemned; he has crossed over from death to life" (John 5:24).

What does it mean to believe in God's Son? Can we pick and choose which miracles he performed that we sort of feel are valid? Should we say, "I like this teaching, but I disagree with that one. It doesn't resonate with me. It's not my thinking. Sorry, Jesus, but I can only embrace part of what you tell us."? If we do, we overlook the hard fact that he proved to be the greatest realist of all time. His miracles and teachings don't represent a buffet in which we select only what we like. He spoke with authority, even declaring that *he himself* is the truth (John 14:6). Plus, he never mixed his message with deception.

Jesus's resurrection leads to grace, and many people are smart enough not to reject it. "It is by grace that you have been saved, through faith—and this is not from yourselves, it is a gift from God—not by good works, so that no one can boast" (Ephesians 2:8–9). Let's not hand back a great gift from God. By sending his Son, God opened up heaven for anyone who desires to receive grace. Jesus loved people so much that he died in our place to pay our debt of sin so that we can be forgiven. It's no wonder there's a well-known, still-popular song called "Amazing Grace." God always wants us to be with him forever.

Good People Can Fool Us

✦

We have all known helpful, friendly, kind human beings who have come through for us at critical times. The goodness they exude appears to be about equal to that of a Christian. These people are seemingly well-adjusted, giving, compassionate folk—in other words, just the kind of people you would pick out as the most trustworthy from your local church. Only one thing is missing: they are nonbelievers.

Sometimes, such a person leaves us stunned because we can't help but say to ourselves, "Wow, he's [she's] a better man [woman] than I am." How do we handle this aggravating contradiction? What do we have left to say to fine people who have sacrificed for us but who don't know much about Jesus?

First of all, anyone on earth can do a good deed, no matter the individual's life history. Thankfully, God gave us a conscience, and sometimes, we actually listen to it and show our best side. We can't expect unbelievers to be *all* bad any more than a Christian can be *all* good, all day long. That's simply a fact of life. This precious conscience we possess allows us to discern basic good and evil. It gives us a head start on the pathway toward perceiving God's *perfect* goodness.

Moreover, what we really want to know is this: "Are many non-Christians actually just as good as Christians? That would be surprising and defeating if it's true." And here we have Jesus commanding us, "Unless your righteousness surpasses that of the Pharisees and the teachers of the law, you will certainly not enter the kingdom of heaven" (Matthew 5:20). More pressure yet!

So on what basis does God judge us as believers? It's our trust in Christ and his willingness to suffer and die to pay for our sins. We have to repent because no one will enter heaven unforgiven. We can try to keep up with the Joneses by doing many helpful things for others, but in the end, they just might do more. That may look good on the outside, but God is much more concerned that we receive his Son.

We need to be saved first and then allow God to use us to serve him. We should be sold out to the Lord, using our gifts to strengthen and encourage people throughout the years. However, loving our neighbors is never meant to be a contest to see who can love the best or the most. It's simply the outpouring of our hearts because God loves us "so much" (John 3:16). No scoresheet is ever needed.

Years ago, Bill Gates pledged to give away half of his money to charitable causes. He even got many other billionaires to agree to do the same. Every day, Gates gives away a million dollars or more. This means that in twenty-four hours, he will do more good works than we will ever do in our entire lifetimes—if we choose to look at it that way. Such a man might seem well-deserving of heaven, but without Jesus in his life, will he get there? We don't end up telling God, "Hey, listen, I've been a good person, so let me in."

Sometimes we lionize unbelievers who inspire us with their selfless actions. They can cause us to think that they don't really need God all that much. We tend to back off from them. However, we really need to spend *more time* with them! That's called *friendship evangelism*. After a while, we will begin to see chinks in their armor. We will notice sins in their lives of which they are blind because of pride. And pride turns out to be the usual god they will inevitably serve because they don't know the actual living God. Then we will clearly realize the need of so-called good people for Jesus to come into their lives. Such persons may fool us at first, but we don't have to be fooled for long. Everyone needs the Lord!

Did Jesus Really Say that Being Good Won't Get You to Heaven?

These days, many people feel that any person will reach heaven someday if he or she is called *good* by others throughout their lifetimes. A general kind of *goodness* will be sufficient. Actually, no belief in God is even needed. An atheist, a scoffer, a total skeptic, and even those who did almost nothing to help anyone will all arrive in heaven, like it or not, if they are deemed *good people* by enough of their fellow human beings. That's the test; you were decent enough of the time to qualify as a fine person in the eyes of those around you. Simply put, this vague concept of goodness is all that your friends and acquaintances have to go on, which will then lead to the consensus that God, *naturally*, will let you in.

You need not believe in heaven or even desire to go there. You've spent your entire life giving it no thought. Yet in the end, God will certainly say, "You're qualified. You're allowed to enter." You have passed the human litmus test of what's acceptable and what's not. According to human standards, you should make it. According to our own thinking, you've earned it, you deserve it, you have a generally decent heart, and you will be rewarded forever. Apparently, usually, you've tried to do the right thing, and that's all anyone can expect. We perceive that you've done more good works than bad works, and even if not, your excellent deeds were more impactful than your selfish deeds. At least 51 percent of the time, you performed well, or at least your heart was in the right place. You now merit favor upon death.

Maybe all this sounds okay on the surface, but what if God doesn't view things the way that we do? Does God's thinking always have to line up with ours? Isn't saying "Surely God will agree with my feelings about life after death" a bit presumptuous? Perhaps it's called *pretending and speculating*, which avoids the reality of the existence of One who really does understand eternity. Jesus Christ came to earth from his heavenly home and knows everything about the place. Many times he said that God *sent* him. Since Jesus definitely doesn't lie, it would be extremely wise to just listen to him.

Jesus doesn't tell us that heaven is filled with people who were *good enough* to get in. Nor does he say that there are those who gave away all their money to the poor or did countless acts of kindness and, therefore, earned everlasting life. He doesn't even say that some people barely made it, as they squeaked through the entrance before God could change his mind. In fact, Jesus doesn't even validate our own preconceived ideas of how we deserve to be welcomed into heaven because we tried so hard to be good and do good. That's not his thinking at all.

Instead of telling us what fine human beings we are, Jesus proclaims, "Repent and believe the good news" (Mark 1:15). Then he startles us by declaring, "No one is good—except God alone" (Luke 10:18). And just when we'd like him to reassure us about our heavenly future, he bluntly states, "Enter through the narrow gate. For wide is the gate and broad is the road that leads to destruction, and *many* enter through it. But small is the gate and narrow is the road that leads to life, and only a *few* find it" (Matthew 7:13–14). Jesus loves us enough that he speaks the truth, though it can alter our mindset.

He wasn't done. At the Last Supper, he holds up the cup, saying, "This is my blood, which is poured out for you for the forgiveness of sins" (Matthew 26:28). He often uses the word *sin* as he informs us of our true standing before God. We might think this term is archaic, but even the Lord's Prayer implores us to ask God to "forgive us our sins" (Matthew 6:12). Jesus wasn't here to let us know how good we already are. In no way should he ever be considered an addition or an upgrade to a life already well lived. We desperately need to surrender our prideful ways to him and not let our own inventive ideas about the afterlife blind us. Let's listen to the Son of God as he reveals who he is: "For my Father's will is that everyone who *looks* to the Son and *believes* in him shall have *eternal life*" (John 6:40). Good news!

The Biggest Mistake Ever

The Bible has a word to describe those who scoff at the idea that there is a God. In fact, the Bible uses the same word twice in Psalm 14 and Psalm 53. Each time, such a person is told exactly what he has become—a *fool*. More specifically, "The fool says in his heart, 'There is no God'" (Psalms 14:1, 53:1). That's a straightforward declaration with no soft pedaling.

Let's take a look at the future of a person who believes that the Bible's words are *true*. If that individual passes away and it turns out that there is no God and no heaven, he loses nothing. However, if an unbeliever dies and then discovers that there really *is* a God *and* a heaven, he loses everything. Are you the first person or the second one? God continually urges us to choose wisely, for life doesn't end here.

Personally, I don't desire to end up being the *fool* that the Bible describes. That would be the biggest mistake and the dumbest I could ever make. Why would I choose to never pray or to say the word *god* to anyone or to thank him for anything whatsoever? Why pick such an empty, hollow approach to life? Jesus did not endure agonizing pain on the cross only to see us react with, "I don't care."

Some people honestly believe that their feistiness will prevent God from ever judging them. In other words, if they act ornery and set in their ways, then God will simply back off and let them be stubborn. He won't want much to do with them. The hardcore resistance they display toward God will cause him to say, "I think I'll just leave those people alone." Of course, nothing could be farther from the truth. God is not scared off by anyone's toughness and defiance. He sees right through us and never gives up on us. On the other hand, if we really don't want him in our lives, he will actually permit us to have it our way. When we reject God, he can't and won't force us to trust in him and will allow us to live out our eternal lives without him. That's called separation from God or *hell* in the Bible. And it's *our* choice.

Now the *good person* question comes along. Here's the typical statement: "Look, I'm just trying to be a good person. I do the best I can. I help people, I'm kind to my family, I work hard, I come home at night, I play with my kids, I give to charities, I donate my efforts to good causes, and I don't cheat or hurt anyone. So stop bugging me about admitting my sins, needing to be forgiven, looking into the Bible, or having a *personal relationship* with Jesus Christ. I'm already trying to be the best fellow I can be. I've got a lot on my plate and don't have much extra time. Sunday is my only day off, and I need to relax."

Gosh, that sounds convincing! Who would want to risk agitating this man or woman? I used to be that individual in many ways. Around 1980, I thought I was a really nice, pleasant guy. People thought so too! But I knew that inside of me, something wasn't right. I wasn't right. There's a God-shaped void or vacuum inside all our bodies. It's a hole in our hearts if you will. I could sense it. I had heard of the God of the Bible, I knew about Jesus, and I could tell that I was far from them both. Most of all, I could see that I was lost, even though I appeared to be a wonderful person. That's quite possible, believe me.

God took my wayward state and turned me back to him. I realized, deep down, that I needed a closer tie with my heavenly Father. Outwardly, you can be a fine member of society, and inwardly, an angry, rebellious individual toward Jesus, who suffered and died to forgive your sins. You may say you don't feel a need for him and that you're not missing anything. I say that you, therefore, are on the verge of being lost forever. Earthly life is short, but eternal life is long, especially when cut off from the One who loves you. So cry out to God. Ask him to save you. You are quite lost without the Lord each day. Simply turn off all TVs and phones and tell God how sorry you are you have put him last in your life. His love and forgiveness will fill your heart as nothing else will. His cleansing Spirit will bring you lasting peace.

Fatalism and Free Will

Frequently, people believe that their lives are scripted ahead of time, and they are resigned to follow the script. Their parents turned out a certain way and so they will turn out the same way. Or they were raised to embrace particular beliefs and that means they will uphold those beliefs for their entire lives. Or the career they choose will be similar to their parents' careers. Very little can be altered because it is nearly impossible to change a script that is already etched in stone. How we were taught will make us who we are now, and nothing can be done about it.

The pressure to conform to the patterns of life laid down before us will always be too strong to resist. This approach to living is called *fatalism*. I call it *giving up and giving in* as well. Who says that all of us will inevitably reach a predetermined identity due to our upbringing? And who decides that we might as well give up trying to think differently from those who were closest to us in our formative years? I don't agree with that reasoning for one minute.

We can respond intentionally and proactively throughout our lives if we choose. We have been given a gift from God which enables us to question the past and to employ our reasoning skills. That gift is free will. Some call it free choice. At every moment, we can use it for good or evil. We can also choose who we want to become even as we turn our thoughts toward spiritual matters. Nobody made us robots.

If we were born into a nonreligious home in which the word *god* was rarely spoken, except, perhaps, in cursing, that doesn't mean we submissively say, "Well, that's just how I was raised. Since my parents expressed no belief in a Supreme Being, then I'll simply walk in their footsteps." That should never be the case. We need not acquiesce and conclude that we were brought up one way, so we'll live each day that same way, and we'll surely die clinging to that way. Can't we think independently outside the box?

The God of the Bible often promises to make all things new. Furthermore, any person is able to become "a new creation" (2 Corinthians 5:17). Even more powerful is Jesus's claim that "if the Son sets you free, you will be free indeed" (John 8:36). Jesus exists as our greatest living example to follow, and God himself wants to impact our lives and radically remake us. How? Only by entering our hearts. For each one of us, that means an exciting, joyful experience called "the new birth" (1 Peter 1:3) can take place. It dramatically softens the cold, hardened heart we may have never known we possess. Yes, God says we have always existed with such a heart until we come to him. Then the Holy Spirit will change us.

Since we are given the gift of free will, it's not impossible to check out this new life God offers us. Far mightier than free will is the awesome gift of grace. God is emphatically explaining through his word that "all people have sinned and fall short of the glory of God" (Romans 3:23). However, "if we confess our sins, he is faithful and just and will forgive us and purify us from all unrighteousness" (1 John 1:9). He desires to forgive, to extend undeserved grace, and even promises us eternal life in heaven with him. That's the best news ever but only if we will accept and receive his sinless Son, Jesus Christ. This man suffered and died for our wrongs so that we are made righteous before the Lord. Without Jesus taking our place on the cross, we have no hope of heaven or of ever having a right relationship with God.

"If you confess with your mouth that 'Jesus is Lord,' and believe in your heart that God raised him from the dead, then you will be saved'" (Romans 10:9–10). By letting go of our pride, talking humbly to God, and accepting his loving invitation to be saved by grace, we will break the chains binding us to the past. For Christ tells us, "No one is good—except God alone" (Luke 18:19). We need a Savior, and no one ever made that claim for himself except Jesus. He's the biggest life changer of all time! Will you repent, as I had to do, then be born again, become a new creation, and receive a new heart? I pray that you will.

Be Intentional about Your Life

Many men don't plan for the future. Often, their entire social lives are tied to their jobs. Men's identities are closely related to success at work, and some of that is a good thing. However, men are considered *lone wolves* by psychologists, and that's not good. Men instinctively know that they must become excellent providers, even if they are required to put in many extra hours. However, they will often do just what is required, as far as relationships are concerned, in order to cultivate an image of affability without attachment. In other words, the norm is, "It's best to be friendly but distant." Therefore, fellow employees usually do not become friends for life. It is left for the wives to develop such close bonds with others because that is their traditional role and strength. Guys, for the most part, want to come home at day's end and simply relax, most often with family, but not with outsiders.

What is the outcome of a lifelong absence of close, visible friends? (This does not include social media contacts.) The end result is that upon retirement, usually in his sixties, a man can quickly find himself alone. Close ties to his job are rapidly severed. A man can return to visit his former employment site a couple of times, but after that, it will seem odd to ever come back. He is quite suddenly left with no groups, no personal friends, little social life, and very few conversations. Studies have shown that this kind of existence is bad for the brain and bad for the body as well. Deterioration will gradually set in, perhaps imperceptibly, and a few years later, a very different human being will emerge.

This new man will have accepted his new status as a senior without question, and he will believe that nothing could or should be done to change it. This is the way that the golden years are meant to be; there's no alternative, so let's just get on with it. The television is turned on much more frequently, and the characters on the screen sometimes become substitute friends. Staying indoors most of the day becomes part of the routine because, over time, the outside world seems less and less necessary to deal with. Relationships suffer and simply disappear because relating to people was mostly a requirement of the work world. It was never a conscious idea. It never became a question of "What do I really want in terms of friendships?" And for many guys, they never stop to figure out what they truly *do* need for a healthy social life. Often, they simply follow along passively, if and when their wives decide to ask over another couple. For men to be proactive in this area would seem absurdly out of character.

This is a negative scenario! Is there any way out? What can a man do to alter an unstimulating, isolating future of increased television viewing? Can he create a course of action for his present life that will help him down the road? The answer is a resounding *yes!*

He must realize that he needs to develop strong friendships right now. Trying to do so at age sixty-five will be challenging although it's never too late. He needs to join a group, the sooner the better, regardless of how tough the work week is. He needs to invite other men to go out for breakfast or lunch. He needs lengthy, sit-down, invigorating discussions above and beyond the usual small talk required just to fit in. Certainly this includes men outside his family who may lack a close friend as well. More importantly, he must decide that passivity is not a manly trait, and that being intentional will help him to live a richer, fuller life. A man needs a plan, and it's never too early to start one. Putting it off by declaring, "I'll take life as it comes" will only allow poor habits to set in, such as avoiding live social contact. By the time the senior years arrive, these habits will be deeply ingrained. Coupled with the human tendency toward shyness and suddenly, a man will no longer engage in enough meaningful conversations on a daily basis.

Guys ask, and women do as well, "Okay, where do I find a good group with which to associate? Where can I make some lasting friendships?" Drop the red flags on the ground for a moment and be open now.

Some of the best people you can find will be at your local house of worship. They restore your faith in humanity. The reason why? Most friends or acquaintances might get in touch with you sporadically—perhaps once a month or twice a year. That is not enough for the human spirit. We need more personal connections than that. Members of the faith community show up every seven days. They *reinforce* your confidence in the human race by consistently being ready to receive you warmly and to get to know you on a weekly basis. Very often, there are midweek activities as well. Small groups of eight to ten people meet regularly to talk, learn, and grow. Casual potlucks take place from time to time. Caring individuals build you up spiritually and socially. You need not have an empty spot in your heart and wonder why. You are undergirded with God's strength and with down-to-earth friends who will stay alongside you for life.

Two different times when my wife, Becky, was very sick with cancer, our church sprang into action. Members called us, visited us, and sent cards—but that's not all. In 2011, they signed up to bring dinners to our home practically every night for two months. And in 2017, they did it again. We were greatly encouraged by their compassion, concern, and tender hearts. Did you realize that church people do such things? They certainly do and much more. They continuously and joyfully lift you up and support you in countless ways. Some of us do not know this because we don't trust and we don't reach out and we retreat from the world and it hurts us. We should give folks a chance. We need to receive that kind of love and to give it back as well.

It's true that no group is perfect, and no human being is faultless either. Forgiveness is always called for. Here's a credible thought: we have let people down more than once. We've had to ask them to forgive us and have hoped that they would, even when we really blew it. Therefore, we have to forgive as well. Yes, I just described myself for sure. I strongly hope that many words and actions of mine were forgiven.

Of course, friends can be found in many other places. Who also helped us when we were struggling? Neighbors did again and again. I'll never forget the selfless giving of our friends who went the second mile. They sacrificed their time to help Becky, and I'm forever grateful. My street is the greatest!

This essay is intended for men, but women can isolate just as easily too. That's not a healthy lifestyle, and everyone knows it. Isolating feels safe but is quite destructive to the soul. There is nothing admirable about being determined to stick with the same old familiar routine year after year.

Most of us would agree that it's pretty important to be proactive and intentional about our lives. I've been passive and laid-back far too many times myself, and it got me nowhere. I was simply stuck. Now I've discovered that if we will extend ourselves to people more than ever before, we will enrich our remaining years. We greatly need others, but sometimes, we forget the fact that they very much need us as well. It works both ways. Truthfully, we were not created by God to spend too much time alone.

Higher Power

Is God a higher power? Of course he is! He's the highest one of all. But is that all that he is? Should we stop right there and say, "That's good enough for me"? Maybe we should think about it a little more.

The Bible tells us to call God "our Father." We get that from the Lord's Prayer in Matthew 6:9. Jesus himself told us we can do that, and *he* called him "my Father" as well. So, since Jesus did it, why can't we do the same? If we think of God as our Father, he will become much more personal to us.

Many scriptures tell us that he is really a personal God. This means he cares about us and desires for us to know him. Why should we sell him short? What good does that do for anyone? Since God wants to have a relationship with every single person, we'd be quite foolish not to say, "Yes, I'm in."

Some people are actually afraid of a god like this. They want to keep him at arm's length. It's better if he is impersonal because we don't want the closeness. It makes us uncomfortable. We don't like that idea because it means we might not measure up. That's where love comes in.

Jesus said that God loves us individually. He said it over and over in many ways. Jesus told a great story about a prodigal son in Luke 15. Prodigal means *wasteful*. How about wasteful and *reckless*? This boy asked for his inheritance early on because he wanted to travel far and have a good time. Soon he took off, squandering all his money on wild living and ending up broke. He was afraid to ever go back home, but when he did, his father ran out to meet him and hug him. The family held a huge celebration right away. Jesus was trying to tell us that God is this way. He forgives us and loves us when we turn back to him. How great is that? God is not angry and unapproachable. He wants us to draw close to him.

Some people recoil at the idea of talking to God in their own words, as if God would never listen. We'd rather hand it over to a pastor to do all the talking and leading. It's better to keep a safe distance from God because he might just get mad since you've been away for so long. He could even smack you one.

The truth is that this vengeful, threatening God is not found in Scripture—not since Jesus was sent to this earth. We can talk to our Father throughout the day, and he will listen. He desires for us to let him into our lives at all times. We shouldn't think about him only on Sundays and leave that as the one day when we pray and read some verses. Instead, we can put God first all week long.

My wife's favorite verse was, "Cast all your cares upon him, for he cares for you" (1 Peter 5:7). And one of mine is, "Draw near to the Lord, and he will draw near to you" (James 4:8). We can search out our favorite parts of the Bible by ourselves without someone else doing it for us. Discover the book of John.

Somebody once said, "Christianity is not a religion—it's a relationship." That idea doesn't just sound good—it actually *is* good! Nothing could be more true. Jesus said that the greatest commandment is to "love God with all your heart, all your soul, all your mind, and all your strength" (Mark 12:30). That changes things. You can't love someone who is only an impersonal force to you. Jesus is telling us that our Father has a great love for us that will take us all the way to heaven. We need to love him back with everything we've got and thank him for sending Jesus, who suffered greatly to pay for our sins.

If we have been far from the Lord, we can ask him to forgive us and open up our hearts today. He's waiting for us to get to know him much better right now. Why would we say "no"? Prayer is a two-way conversation between you and God. He's a higher power for sure, but he's also so much more!

Does God Romance Us?

I heard a unique message twenty years ago, but the speaker's name escapes me. In it, he strongly suggested that God is continually wooing and loving us in an all-out effort to win us to himself. He loves us so greatly that he will continuously try to *romance* us into his kingdom. I listened curiously for a while and then started to see what the speaker meant. Slowly, I began to understand his thinking, though I had never heard this kind of explanation. He was saying God's passionate heart will never stop drawing us toward him until we choose to come into his presence. He will persist with even the most hardheaded among us right up to the day we pass away. He desires an intimate relationship with every person, although we usually ignore him. We're too busy; he's not. We stay distant; he remains close. We hope people will meet our needs; he fulfills our hearts' desires. We prefer worldly things; he says, "Come to me." We're continually restless; he satisfies us with true peace. We're afraid to trust him completely; he assures us that he is faithful. We want to tell God who he is; he wants us to know who he *really* is.

Our heavenly Father romances us. In fact, that is probably the greatest action he initiates. Relentlessly, he pursues us with patience and gentleness. He even describes his character perfectly in Jeremiah 31:3, "I have loved you with an everlasting love; I have drawn you with loving-kindness." How could we say "No!" to him after such a verse? He wants us to love him back. That will be the start of our life-long friendship. After all, he invites us to "draw near to the Lord, and he will draw near to you" (James 4:8). He is not a remote, impersonal force. Why think that way when he's just the opposite?

This is the God I met personally at age fourteen. I was reading the Gospel of John one night and became overwhelmed by Jesus's words, deeds, compassion, and strength. Setting the Bible down, I said, "God, I'll do anything for you the rest of my life."

I was reaching out with all I had to give. Right then, this supernatural love, joy, and peace flooded my heart and mind. God was responding with the Holy Spirit washing over me. I realized I was being born again, though I knew very little about such an encounter at the time. After a few minutes, things returned to normal, but I was changed. God had taken up residence in my heart, and I would never be the same. That night has remained with me all these years. God's love won me over. I had wanted to know if he was real, and he answered my request because I accepted his Son, Jesus. Anyone can do that. Anyone can experience the wonderful presence of God.

Along the same lines, I once read a book with words such as these: "Jesus had the most joyful idea of God that ever was." Is that ever true! Even if we have the most difficult life, God's joy will comfort us in our struggles. In fact, "The joy of the Lord is our strength" (Nehemiah 8:10). I can't explain how, but if we put our trust in the God of the Bible, he will fortify us with hope and encouragement throughout our years. He will help us cope with hard times, bringing us through them and overcoming them. I've had many and I know. Joy still remains in me from my youth, and it increases when I build up my faith by praying, reading Scripture, showing up at church, and interacting with Christian friends.

This isn't a philosophy of *looking on the bright side*. No, not at all. It's actually a relationship with my heavenly Father, who romances us and desires for each person to know him. He will be close in trials, tragedies, and temptations. Jesus himself promises, "I will be with you always" (Matthew 28:20). He also assures us, "I have told you all these things so that my joy may be in you and your joy may be full" (John 15:11).

Are you curious about this God whom you perhaps don't yet know? Take a leap of faith and reach out to him. It's an empty life without experiencing God's amazing love. Please realize that he is romancing you and always will until you respond back. He cares deeply about your questions, worries, past history, failures, regrets, and losses. Cry out to him at any time, and he will meet you with an embrace!

God Sent Us a Love Letter

It has been said many times that Christianity is not just a religion—it's a relationship. It has also been said that Jesus is the only founder of a major religion who is still alive! He is the one who seeks a relationship with each and every individual. Perhaps we don't fully realize that forming a bond with the one known as the Son of God will fulfill our lives, but his offer always stands. We have until our last day on earth to make that life-changing decision. The trouble is that we don't know what day that will be. Therefore, it's vital to say "yes" to Jesus today and not procrastinate. Tomorrow is promised to no one.

Truthfully, God doesn't leave us guessing if he's knowable, yet many people spend years debating his mere existence in their minds. Here are some of their typical thoughts: "Well, maybe there's a God." "There's got to be something out there." "I don't know. God seems distant, if he/she even exists at all." "I want to believe, but I just can't." "There has to be a Supreme Being." "No, God's not around." "If I can't see or touch something, then to me, it's not real." "Then who created all of this?" "You can't prove there's a God." "You can't prove there's not a God either." So on and on it goes. However, we need not become mired in a state of uncertainty for our entire lives. There's no need to be a doubter.

God's inspired love letter to everyone is called 1 John. This short book is located in a hard-to-reach portion of the Bible, just before Jude and Revelation. Had it been placed immediately after the *Gospel* of John, we would have become much more familiar with it. After all, both books were written by the same author, the disciple John.

What John does, more than any other writer, is this: if we aren't sure that a living God actually cares about us, he positively and emphatically tells us it's true. *Absolutely* true!

John declares that we can *know* the answers to life's greatest questions. We can "know what love is" because "Jesus Christ laid down his life for us" (1 John 3:16). How awesome and reassuring is that news! Jesus suffered in our place and forgave us out of his perfect love. Our hearts say "Thank you" right now. We should take John seriously, for he was the last living disciple when he wrote his book around AD 90. He knew the Master closely and was known as "the disciple whom Jesus loved" (John 13:23). When Christ was executed, John stood by his cross, comforting Jesus's mother, Mary, to the very end.

John says that all people who believe in God's Son can "know that he (Jesus) lives in us: We know it by the Spirit he gave us" (1 John 3:24). The evidence we seek for God's existence comes invisibly in the form of the Holy Spirit. God enters our hearts when we finally realize that we are sinners and that this wonderful Son of God actually loves and forgives us. We will find that God is truly real because he comes to live inside of us. He places his perfect peace and joy within us, and we will know him deeply. We become "born again" (John 3:3) spiritually, and we are now "reconciled" (2 Corinthians 5:18) to God.

We no longer have to wonder if there's a heaven and whether or not we will be going there. John explains what Jesus has done for us, "God has given us eternal life and this life is in his Son. I write these things to you who believe in the name of the Son of God so that you *may know* that you have eternal life" (1 John 5:12–13). John is expressing strong conviction as he points all seekers to the faithful promises of his Savior. God wants us with him forever, for the greatest love is always everlasting love.

First John is only four pages long. There are many other remarkable verses to consider besides the ones quoted above. John makes Jesus's powerful messages clear and inviting. He's sharing first-hand truths. Many people who humbled themselves before God and admitted that they need him have experienced a changed life—a new life. God wants to do so much in our hearts if we will repent of our wrongs and believe in his Son. So love the Lord and ask Jesus to come into your life. Today is the best time!

"Let Someone Else Pray"

I've heard the expression, "Let someone else pray" many times. Often, it occurs at a holiday dinner table when one person is a bit coerced into saying a blessing and shies away. Then somebody else will be asked, and on and on until a reluctant volunteer is finally found. Of course, many families skip the prayer idea altogether, while others will call upon the token Christian at the table to do the honors every year. Still, other families actually have several willing members who love to say grace at any time.

Was praying ever meant to be so difficult in the first place? Billy Graham once said, simply, "Prayer is a two-way conversation between you and God." Graham's idea strikes a reassuring tone, giving us a mental picture of a God who listens lovingly, privately, and intimately. Our words are special to him—as special as we are. If we feel foolish when we pray, God doesn't think so. He loves us whenever we attempt to speak with him. Communication is key to this relationship, and he even welcomes a flowing, running, all-day exchange just between us and himself. Plus, we don't have to say all the right things either.

Once, when I was very troubled, I yelled, "Help me!" about a hundred times as I drove to Pasadena—just those two words. I know that God was listening because he miraculously answered my loud prayer a few years later. He wants us to be real. Psalm 10 begins this way: "Why, O Lord, do you stand far-off? Why do you hide yourself in times of trouble?" Psalm 13 starts off like this: "How long, O Lord? Will you forget me forever?" We can show our true feelings to God, and he will still engage us.

Are memorized prayers pleasing to the Lord? Yes and no. Some people substitute such prayers for the natural contact for which God yearns. The Bible is lengthy, and many pages are filled with his direct words to seekers and believers. Should we think that God wouldn't want us to express our hearts with our very own words in return? We need not be afraid to talk one-on-one concerning anything on our minds. We ought to joyfully praise and thank God as well for all that he faithfully continues to do to bless us each day. Then, we can listen and wait for his answers, for they will come

Sometimes we try so hard to solve problems by ourselves that we forget that even Jesus prayed. The Son of God needed to pray. So what about us? If *he* needed to pray, then what about *us*? The Bible says that Jesus often prayed in "lonely places" (Luke 5:16) and would "spend the night praying to God" (Luke 6:12). Some people pray for a few minutes while others take a few hours. I used to feel inferior to those who spent more time with the Lord until I realized that we're all created differently. He hears me, and he doesn't carry a stopwatch. I may not be a prayer warrior, but I do have a big heart for God.

Indeed, Jesus also taught us the Lord's Prayer. From that prayer, we can gain a strong sense of what's important to God. Yet many of us have often repeated its words without much thought about their content. Let's pause to see what they convey: God resides in heaven; we can call him "Father"; he is holy; his will shall someday prevail on earth as it now does in heaven; we are to thank him for our daily provisions; we are to ask God for forgiveness and forgive others; we are to ask him to lead us away from temptation and to deliver us from Satan, the evil one; and we should gladly exalt the Lord forever with all we've got! The Lord's Prayer is wonderful to memorize or to express in our own way.

Anyone who has wasted as many hours as I have on meaningless, ridiculous activities will appreciate a verse from a well-known poem. A century ago, the English missionary, Charles Thomas Studd, wrote, "Only one life, 'twill soon be past, Only what's done for Christ will last." If we choose to serve God and to grow in faith, then we will have chosen wisely. Ephesians 6:18 captures our need to reach out to our heavenly Father: "And pray in the Spirit on all occasions with all kinds of prayers and requests." Who knows? By developing a love for praying, we may even wind up with a strong desire to say a blessing at the dinner table! People will actually be listening, and God will surely be working.

"I Can Forgive, but I Can't Forget"

When I was younger, I would hear this title repeated fairly often. Mostly, what I remember now is the final word *forget*. It always landed like a thud in my spirit, causing me to question whether or not the people who spoke it actually intended to forgive anybody at all. Of course, it's impossible for any person to simply forget having been treated badly, but forgiveness can definitely be life changing and freeing.

I rarely hear the phrase anymore. Why would anyone use it when he or she can always take out frustrations and seek revenge through social media? There's no reason to forgive *or* forget these days. You simply keep on posting and venting week after week. Perhaps very few will thoughtfully read what you write, but somehow, you get to feel important. It's sort of like yelling into a strong headwind.

Forgive is a formidable word not to be taken lightly. A person has to be careful how and when to say it. During my thirty-nine years of teaching, I had to settle many arguments among children. In working them out, I would never attempt to ask one child to forgive the offending one. Such a term seemed too strong and almost too religious. I would seldom hear other teachers try it with their own students too. However, I now believe *forgiveness* could have been a powerful tool for reducing anger all along.

Having been kicked out of two different homes without warning at ages twelve and nineteen, I had to look into myself and ask how I was going to respond to sudden rejections. You see, I never saw those houses again. I lost my friends, my schools, my pets, and my security all in ten minutes before being whisked away each time—

that's how long I was given to pack a suitcase. I was thoroughly evicted, not to return.

Surprisingly, I hardly ever felt mad—just mostly sad. Eventually, I saw the good that came out of each rejection. God used those instances to bring me closer to him and to Christian friends who would love me unconditionally. It took years, but I finally grasped the truth: "And we know that in all things God works for the good of those who love him" (Romans 8:28). Still, to this day, I have to guard against false fears that creep up on me of being left out or overlooked. I'm not completely healed—we never are.

Sometimes, in small group Bible studies, this question is posed: "How can we begin to forgive others who have hurt us?" Many excellent, biblical answers are offered by members, and I agree with each one: "Jesus forgave all of us from the cross." "God loves us so much that he even gave his own Son to suffer and pay for our sins." "God himself is long-suffering." "Jesus said to forgive 'seventy times seven,' which means *infinitely*" (Matthew 18:22). Then, I often add these thoughts to the conversation: "It's not always a question of forgiving others but of realizing that we desperately desire for people whom we've offended over the years to forgive *us*. At least *I do*! Maybe we forget that. It certainly makes it easier for me to be forgiving when I think about all the offenses I've committed toward others."

Many of us can recite the Lord's Prayer, but the very next verse that follows it bears mentioning. Jesus went on to declare, "If you forgive others when they sin against you, your heavenly Father will forgive your sins. But if you do not forgive others, your heavenly Father will not forgive your sins" (Matthew 6:14–15). That sounds like a stern warning to me. How can I not surrender my critical feelings toward several individuals I know to the Lord and confess my guilt for breaking one of Jesus's clear teachings?

Yes, many people need years of counseling and therapy to help overcome their pasts. Any number of unresolved childhood conflicts are still resurfacing, even at the same time that new adult issues have arisen. It's a slow, difficult process, especially for abuse victims. I can only share that Jesus Christ set me on the path of mercy, empathy, and compassion. Without him entering my world, I would have ended up a bitter man, unable to grow. He changed my heart and thought life, replacing deep sorrow with joy! I can forgive without venom through the power of his perfect love. He will change your own life as well.

Why Do We Limit God?

When someone looks up the definition of God on the internet, he or she will find the words *Creator*, *ruler*, and *the Supreme Being*. Not surprisingly, these are the exact words we would expect. Even without being defined, the very word *god* denotes the ultimate cosmic force, separate from mankind.

Some people believe that God *does* exist, but about all he does is answer a prayer once in a while. He's not much more than an inert, passive entity, who, perhaps, created everything, sent the planets into orbit, but then kicked back and said, "Okay, it's up to you now. I've done my part already." He's sort of like a benign, grandfatherly figure in the sky who watches over us with a faint smile throughout the day. He seldom reacts, he hardly moves, he doesn't relate to anyone, but he likes to give little pats on the head. In short, he's a supernatural being who can't do anything supernatural. We won't let him.

Where did we come up with a limited concept of God such as this? We're saying that God cannot enter or influence our physical realm because his actions would violate the laws of nature. God himself is restricted from intervening in the universe which he created. To do so would upset the orderliness and predictability of daily living. So we've put God in a box, and we'll keep him there, just in case, and we don't want any trouble. That way, we can avoid all interference in our lives.

This is not the God I've known. He's exactly the opposite of everything written above. All that anyone has to do is to let him have a chance and then accept the possibility that we have wrongly prejudged our Creator. His power is truly *unlimited,* and his desire for every person to worship him is constant.

If God doesn't do much at all, then why am I a changed person? Did I improve myself through the gradual maturation process? Hardly! Only God could have redeemed me from a slow slide into hell. He saved my very soul by helping me, even when I paid him no attention, by chastening me when nothing else would work, and by revealing himself through the God-man, Jesus Christ, whom I came to admire. He continued to pursue me when I was lost and would pour out his extraordinary love to draw me close. Finally, he confirmed the truth of scripture: "It is the kindness of God that leads you to repentance" (Romans 2:4). He is so loving that he gave up his own Son to suffer and die, causing me to understand that I really needed a Savior. At long last, I was convicted enough to openly admit, "Sorry, God. I'm so sorry that I've been sinning against you. It takes a whole lot to give up your own Son, especially your 'one and only Son'" (John 3:16).

If what I shared doesn't touch your heart, then perhaps you've allowed yourself to become spiritually dead. How will you enter heaven without a right standing with the Lord? Good deeds won't be enough, for Jesus tells us, "No one is good—except God alone" (Mark 10:18). Surrender your life to the Lord, seek his overflowing forgiveness, and let him fill you with the Holy Spirit. Turn from your indifference toward him. Don't listen to others who live their lives ignoring him. God warns us not to harden our hearts. My tears for you right now reflect the goodness that God himself has shown me. He's personal and relational, and he wants you to know him through his Son. Grab a Bible, read the astonishing book of John, and discover all that you didn't realize about Jesus, the greatest man in history.

That's my reality-based advice. No logical proofs presented. No astute arguments. No emotional appeals. Just give Jesus the biggest opportunity you've ever permitted him, and he won't let you down. God bless you. God does actually love you intimately. Therefore, the Bible says, "Humble yourselves before the Lord, and he will lift you up" (James 4:10). Jesus is not simply a helpful addition to a life already well lived. He's the ultimate game changer.

About the Author

Charlie Burr was born in 1949 in Berkeley, California. He earned a BA in speech and a California teaching credential from California State University, Northridge, in 1974. He soon began a long career as an elementary physical education specialist. That same year, he married Becky Comstock, his college sweetheart. Their marriage lasted forty-three years until she passed away from cancer in 2017. Becky was a wonderful elementary school teacher for most of her adult life. Together, they had one son, Jason Burr, now forty, who visits his dad every week!

Charlie tutors students in math, reading, and language arts and has enjoyed his pet dog and cats at his house in Los Angeles, California. He attends nearby Calvary Chapel LAX. Charlie started writing four years ago and hopes that this collection of his work will inspire and awaken you to the possibility of encountering God. Each meaningful composition was written with you, the reader, foremost in mind. Eight personal stories are presented first, followed by thirty-four short, insightful essays. All Bible quotations are taken from the New International Version, 1978.

Please enjoy this unique reading experience, and feel free to share some of Charlie's writings with anyone you know.

February 1, 2023